Transforming
Learning
With Block
Scheduling

CORWIN PRESS

The **Corwin Press logo**—a raven striding across an open book—represents the happy union of courage and learning. We are a professional-level publisher of books and journals for K–12 educators, and we are committed to creating and providing resources that embody these qualities. Corwin's motto is "Success for All Learners."

Transforming Learning With Block Scheduling

A Guide for Principals

Blair Lybbert

CORWIN PRESS, INC.
A Sage Publications Company
Thousand Oaks, California

For information address:

Corwin Press, Inc.
A Sage Publications Company
2455 Teller Road
Thousand Oaks, California 91320
E-mail: order@corwinpress.com

SAGE Publications Ltd.
6 Bonhill Street
London EC2A 4PU
United Kingdom

SAGE Publications India Pvt. Ltd.
M-32 Market
Greater Kailash I
New Delhi 110 048 India

Printed in the United States of America

Library of Congress Cataloging-in-Publication Data

Lybbert, Blair.
   Transforming learning with block scheduling: A guide for principals / by Blair Lybbert.
       p. cm.
   Includes bibliographical references.
   ISBN 0-8039-6657-1 (cloth : acid-free paper)
   ISBN 0-8039-6658-X (pbk. : acid-free paper)
   1. Block scheduling (Education)—United States. I. Title.
LB3032.2 .L93 1998
371.2'42—ddc21   98-9075

98 99 00 01 02 03 10 9 8 7 6 5 4 3 2 1

Editorial Assistant: Julia Parnell
Production Editor: Michèle Lingre
Production Assistant: Karen Wiley
Typesetter/Designer: Marion Warren
Cover Designer: Tracy Miller

Contents

Preface

The very nature of decision making in schools has changed dramatically in the last decade. We have seen a fundamental shift from top down decision making to a process that reaches out to a wide cross section of stakeholders. In some instances, this shared leadership has been mandated, but for the most part educators have come to realize that there are many pieces to the puzzle we call education. Districts that have not yet undertaken an evaluation of block scheduling for their secondary schools almost certainly will in the near future. This book will be a valuable resource as administrators, school leadership teams, and other members of the school community seek to determine if restructuring the use of instructional time can make a contribution to improving their schools. The information offered in this book will be widely applicable even though it is primarily analyzed from a high school perspective. Middle schools and junior high schools will find the principles discussed, and illustrations outlined, to be highly relevant to their reform efforts.

Transforming Learning With Block Scheduling is written by a principal who has been strategically involved in implementing this change in two high schools. This is a practical guide that should help decision makers understand the available options from the many competing scheduling models. In addition, it can be instrumental in helping administrators through the pitfalls of implementing the change. Unlike much of the material available about block scheduling that has been written from an academic perspective, the material in this book combines an academic understanding of block scheduling with the knowledge that flows from the day-to-day experience of a practitioner.

One particularly useful section of the book is the information that will enable administrators to respond to the criticisms they may encounter while investigating, and later implementing, block scheduling. It is only recently that reformers have found that some of the basic principles supporting block scheduling are being challenged by critics. Months of thoughtful work can be delayed by a small number of opponents in critical positions who are bolstered by a few misleading sources of information. Chapter 8 will outline some of the key objections and explain why they lack validity in the overall debate.

The first half of the book will prove invaluable to understanding what a block schedule is and how it organizes the reallocation of instructional time in schools. Even members of a leadership team that might not have a background in educational reform will have a good working knowledge of block scheduling after reading Chapters 2, 3, 4, and 5. Administrators who are familiar with block scheduling should develop a more comprehensive understanding of the models and their variations. In these chapters, you will find detailed descriptions and illustrations of a variety of scheduling models. The problems associated with the various block scheduling models are discussed, and suggestions are made that should resolve issues related to the efficacy of each plan.

The reader will find useful information in Chapter 6 explaining how to begin and follow through in facilitating the various stages of the implementation process. The steps for developing an effective plan of action will be reviewed, and a case study will outline the experience of a South Carolina high school as they implemented block scheduling. In Chapter 7, the focus is on priority decisions necessary to make the transition successful. A survey of principals who have had experience with block scheduling describes what they consider to be the most serious problems they encountered in their schools.

One of the chapters that will provide planners with guidance in trying to structure a working schedule is Chapter 9. This chapter provides numerous sample schedules drawn from schools using alternating blocks, accelerated blocks, modified blocks, and trimester plans. These sample schedules will provide an excellent foundation for planners to structure a schedule to meet the needs of an individual campus. Or, planners may want to select another school's proven formula.

This book is designed and developed to take the reader through the process of block scheduling from the point of interest in the reform to the point of evaluating its effectiveness after several years in place. It is about reforming our schools and how to nurture the spirit of change that makes reform a dynamic process to improve our schools and thereby maximize the opportunities for our children.

Blair Lybbert
Burleson, Texas

About the Author

Blair Lybbert is the principal of Rio Vista High School in Rio Vista, Texas. Mr. Lybbert has been in public school education at the secondary level for 26 years, the last eight as an administrator. He holds a Master's Degree from Texas Christian University. Prior to entering administration, he was a highly successful high school debate coach while also teaching government and speech communication. Mr. Lybbert has published more than a dozen articles in state and national journals and has written several debate analysis and research handbooks. During the last several years, his publications have focused on topics related to educational reform. Mr. Lybbert has been involved in implementing block scheduling in two high schools during the last 5 years and is frequently asked to consult with schools initiating the reform process.

1

The Need to Improve
Our Schools

Reform Movement

The pace of educational reform during the past several decades has been extraordinary. As parents and other taxpayers have become alarmed by media emphasis on the declining quality in America's public schools, the public has begun to demand that schools be more accountable. Indeed, those involved in district and campus level leadership would agree that measurable accountability standards have become the single most defining requirement driving the reform movement of the 1990s.

When *A Nation at Risk* was published in 1983, it focused the public's attention on a wide range of concerns in public education (U.S. Department of Education, 1983). In reality, although the report garnered media attention with inflammatory references to schools so lacking in quality that their imposition on America by a foreign power would be tantamount to an act of war, the commitment to educational improvement has always been a priority concern for those responsible for educating our children. Our schools have grown and changed continuously as they have become more inclusive and more responsive to the public over the years. However, even though schools have improved in many ways, particularly in providing services to previously neglected populations, the fact remains that both internal and external stakeholders in the educational community are seeking solutions to some troubling questions.

Several quality indicators seem to support the proposition that the schools are not making good use of the billions of dollars allocated for education at the local, state, and national levels. SAT scores have been essentially flat or in actual decline for decades even though spending for education has increased significantly during the same time period. A 1995 study by the Economic Policy Institute "reports an increase of about 60 percent in real per-pupil spending, again after adjusting for inflation, from 1967 to 1991" (cited in Anderson, 1997, p. 6). Although some have suggested that poor student performance on the SATs results from the increased number of test takers, it appears that these results cannot be attributed solely to this increase. Education critic Charles Sykes pointed out that "the academic crisis is not confined to low-achieving students. Besides the overall drop, the SAT scores show evidence of rot at the top—a decline in the number of high scoring students" (Sykes, 1995, p. 17).

When our students are compared to those of other industrialized nations, the results have been disappointing. John E. Chubb and Terry M. Moe observed that "American students consistently did worse, often dramatically and embarrassingly worse, than foreign students on internationally standardized tests" (Chubb & Moe, 1990, p. 8). Concerns about the quality of education are not limited to high school students. The National Assessment of Educational Progress (NAEP) tracks student achievement on NAEP tests in math, science, reading, and writing. The testing includes students from the elementary, middle, and high school age groups and provides a long-term measure of student performance. The data reveal that student achievement has been marginal at best and in decline in several areas when traced back to the 1970s and 1980s ("Mixed Bag," 1997, p. 10). And President Clinton claimed in his State of the Union Address that "40 percent of our 8-year-olds cannot read on their own" (Clinton, 1997, p. 4).

It is easy to understand why Americans are increasingly expecting greater accountability for the more than $300 billion annually spent on our schools. Certainly the reform movement of the 1980s and 1990s has been sensitive to the criticisms leveled at the public schools. School districts have adopted a variety of strategies to improve quality. Among the more notable efforts were attempts to implement outcome-based education, total quality management principles, Glasser's quality schools program, merit pay and career ladders for teachers, the whole language movement, and legislatively mandated accountability standards. So many efforts at improvement have been tried in recent years that teachers often refer to new ideas as the "trend of the month."

In Texas in the 1990s, the emphasis has been focused on accountability standards in elementary, middle, and high schools as measured by standardized tests in reading, writing, and math. This Academic Excellence Indicator System also requires data on drop-out rates, attendance, SAT and ACT scores, as well as other factors. The state examinations are constructed under the auspices of the Texas Education Agency and strict guidelines must be followed on testing and data reporting. When the state reports the results back to the schools, the data are disaggregated by grade level, economic status, race, and gender, and by a learning index that compares student progress over the years. All the general data are made available to the media, and districts are required by law to report their results in an open forum with their communities. Many other states have adopted and implemented similar programs based on objective measures of student success. There is little question that there is a significant commitment around the country to find solutions to the problems facing the schools.

As reformers have sought better ways to utilize resources, it was logical to consider the question of how time is used in the instructional day. Unlike some strategies, such as increasing the number of school days or incorporating more technology, better use of available time does not require any addit al expenditure of funds. Educators began to challenge the that the traditional six- or seven-period day was the b rganize class time.

Prob   Traditional Scheduling

The tradition   edule has typically featured six or
seven classes of a   minutes in length offered each
day. Teachers wou   class period off for planning
and conferences. If   periods a day, six instructional, and an avera   ents, then a teacher might
have as many as 15   ay. To state that this is an enor-
mous teaching load   the obvious.

One of the first serious problems encountered with an excessive teaching load is exhaustion on the part of the student and the teacher. We expect teachers to be effective in dealing with large numbers of students while accommodating different learning styles, students with special education modifications that are mandated by their Individual Education Plans (IEPs). We also expect them to handle all the normal dynamics and distractions found in any classroom containing 25 or more students. Special education requirements are particularly significant because most schools have implemented inclusion programs that have special education students in the regular classroom to the greatest extent possible. Teachers and administrators are highly accountable for modifications of the curriculum for each of these students in the class. Failure to follow the provisions of the IEP can create an atmosphere of conflict with parents and even expose the school to civil liability. The ability of a teacher to individualize instruction for 150 students in 50-minute classes is simply unrealistic. Joseph Carroll pointed out that "teachers cannot deal meaningfully with every student every day under this traditional schedule" (Carroll, 1994, p. 27).

From the student's perspective, the problem may be just as bad. Students find themselves moving from one class to another six or seven times each day. Because teachers in shorter classes tend to rely more heavily on the lecture format, a student may find himself or herself a captive audience in a very long day. And the day may be lengthened even more if the student is involved in after school athletics or other cocurricular activities. Students taking advanced classes will probably have several homework assignments as well as the possibility of studying for several tests. The pace can be overwhelming, and most principals working under traditional schedules could, no doubt, recount any number of stories of students dropping advanced courses just to lighten their academic load.

Another important quality-of-time issue relates directly to the number of available instructional minutes. Regardless of the length of the class, some routine procedures must be completed in each class, and when the class is only 50 minutes rather than 90 minutes long, every lost minute takes on added significance. As Osbourne High School Principal Marian B. Stephans claimed, "Studies show that the average 45- to 50-minute class only provides 15 to 18 minutes of educational instruction after you factor in taking attendance, passing out information, giving instructions and handing out restroom passes" (Odum, 1993, p. B1).

In addition to the repetitious loss of time in the class is the time lost to passing periods. Under a traditional schedule, the passing periods alone can consume up to 10% of the school day. This is lost time by anyone's account, and even supporters of the traditional schedule understand that it contributes to a frenzied learning environment.

Block Scheduling as an Alternative

The basic idea of a block schedule is easy to understand. It replaces the traditional class period of approximately 50 minutes with a longer class length, usually one of 90 minutes per class. Instead of six or seven periods the block schedule typically has four periods a day. Oftentimes, scheduling difficulties will find planners modifying this simple approach by adding a short period that meets every day, usually to accommodate athletics, band, or other activities. When considering a block schedule, you need to remember that there are no hard and fast rules that dictate how you organize your time unless those are imposed by state or local policies. Certainly, there are many possible variations of block scheduling; however, the two most common configurations are the alternating block (often referred to as the A/B block) and the accelerated block (often referred to as the 4 × 4 plan).

The alternating block is based on eight class periods each semester in which a student attends periods one through four on one day (A day) and periods five through eight the next day (B day). The student schedule remains the same for the entire year for year-long courses. A student would complete a year-long course by attending that class every other day in both the fall and spring semesters. Students would earn eight credits a year.

The accelerated block also utilizes four 90-minute class periods in its most widely used form. The accelerated block features only four classes each semester, and the student attends each class every day instead of alternating periods from day to day. A student would complete a full year course in one semester and would begin a new course in the spring. Because the student completes four courses in the fall and four courses in the spring, that student has spent the same amount of seat time in each class as students in the alternating block who went to eight classes every other day for the entire year. Students would earn eight credits a year in the accelerated plan.

Although the block scheduling philosophy of extended class periods has been around for many years under other names, such as the Copernican Plan or the quarter system, several factors seem to be contributing to its increasing popularity with school reformers. Obviously, dissatisfaction with the current state of public education provides impetus to almost any idea that offers a potentially better way in which to use instructional time. Edward Miller described the traditional schedule as "inimical to real learning. It fosters lecture style classes that emphasize coverage rather than reflection, discussion, and thoughtful analysis" (Miller, 1992, p. 6). Educators have begun to realize that promoting an organizational structure for the more effective use of available time offers us a tremendous opportunity to enhance the quality of instruction.

Another practical consideration that has prompted the move to block scheduling has been the need to allow students to earn more credits in their graduation plans. In some cases, states have increased the number of required credits for graduation or have provided for advanced/honor graduation plans that include higher standards and additional credits. In other instances, local districts have increased graduation requirements for their students as they implemented goals developed in site-based decision-making teams. Frequently, these local goals reflect the needs of local stakeholder interests and are unique to individual communities. In either case, the traditional schedule is too restrictive to accommodate those needs and allows little flexibility in student scheduling. In the case of students with a schedule of six-period days and higher credit requirements, it becomes virtually impossible to meet those standards and still be able to take elective and enrichment classes and participate in worthwhile activities such as sports or band. As any coach or activity director knows, the student and the program will gain the most when a student can fully participate in an area of high interest and ability for all four years of high school—scheduling should help facilitate such interests.

Block scheduling should be viewed as a means to open up more opportunities for students to add electives, be involved in specialized programs, or even graduate early, as a student would ordinarily earn eight credits each year instead of six or seven. As we will see, there are many other benefits attributed to block scheduling as well as some concerns. One fact is clear, however: Block scheduling is growing in popularity as an educational restructuring strategy.

The undeniable trend in favor of the increased use of block scheduling has become evident during the past several years. Block scheduling workshops at education conferences are still among the best attended, and paid seminars continue to play to large audiences. Among the conclusions reached in Gordon Cawelti's "High School Restructuring: A National Survey," was that block scheduling represented one of the seven most important selected indicators of major restructuring within a school. Cawelti (1994), who conducted the research for the Education Research Service, found that "in addition to about one fourth of responding schools that were already fully (10.9 percent) or partially (12.1 percent) employing this schedule, some 15.4 percent reported that they planned to introduce it during the next school year" (p. 23). In Texas, the Texas Education Agency facilitates information development and distribution from a group of leading high schools called *mentor* schools. These schools are selected through an application process and typically display a strong commitment to leading innovation as well as a proven record of student success. It is not uncommon to see these schools implementing reform strategies several years earlier than most other schools and, of the 40 Texas mentor schools listed, 22 are already using some form of block scheduling. Block scheduling appears to be rapidly gaining momentum as a key component in the movement to reorganize schools for greater student success.

References

Anderson, K. (1997, January). Public school spending: The truth. *The Education Digest*, p. 6.

Carroll, J. M. (1994, March). Organizing time to support learning. *The School Administrator*, p. 27.

Cawelti, G. (1994). *High school restructuring: A national study.* Arlington, VA: Education Research Service.

Chubb, J. E., & Moe, T. M. (1990). *Politics, markets, and America's schools.* Washington, DC: Brookings Institution.

Clinton, W. (1997, April). State of the Union address. *The Education Digest*, p. 4.

Miller, E. (1992, March-April). Breaking the tyranny of the schedule. *The Harvard Education Letter*, p. 6.

Mixed bag for achievement trends. (1997, November). *American School Board Journal*, p. 10.

Odum, M. E. (1993, February 13). Double trouble or twice the fun. *Washington Post*, p. B1.

Sykes, C. J. (1995). *Dumbing down our kids*. New York: St. Martin's.

U.S. Department of Education. (1983). *A nation at risk: The imperative for educational reform*. Washington, DC: National Commission on Excellence in Education.

Suggested Reading

Bennett, W. J. (1992). *The de-valuing of America*. New York: Summit Books.

Canady, R. L., & Rettig, M. D. (1993, December). Unlocking the lockstep high school schedule. *Phi Delta Kappan*, pp. 310-314.

Glatthorn, A. (Ed.). (1995). *Content of the curriculum*. Alexandria, VA: Association for Curriculum and Development.

Johnson, R. C. (1997, November 19). A matter of time: Schools try four-day weeks. *Education Week*.

Ravitch, D. (1995). *National standards in American education*. Washington, DC: Brookings Institution.

Schlechty, P. C. (1991). *Schools for the 21st century*. San Francisco: Jossey-Bass.

Traverso, H. P. (1991, October). Scheduling from micro to macro. *The Practitioner*, pp. 1-8. (NAASP)

Ubben, G. C., & Hughes, L. W. (1987). *The principal*. Boston: Allyn & Bacon.

⊞ 2 ⊞

Understanding the Block

One of the most desirable features of block scheduling is the flexibility it affords decision makers in designing a model that meets the needs of the students in their schools. Although the basic concept of increasing the instructional time of each period and decreasing the number of class periods is relatively simple, the variations on this theme are almost unlimited. The model illustrated in Table 2.1 should be viewed as a starting point.

TABLE 2.1

Period 1 (5)	90 Minutes
Period 2 (6)	90 Minutes
Period 3 (7)	90 Minutes
Lunch	
Period 4 (8)	90 Minutes

Even though there are many possibilities available to planners, caution should be exercised about becoming too creative. The effectiveness of block scheduling in improving schools is built around the premise that "less is more." A class period of 50 minutes in a traditional schedule provides approximately 9,000 minutes of instructional time during the standard 180-day school year. A yearlong blocked course of 90 minutes will provide approximately 8,100 minutes of instructional time. Even taking into account the repeated loss of time for routine tasks over more class periods, most proponents of block scheduling would concede that there will be fewer minutes of actual available class time under virtually any blocking scheme.

To offset the loss of any instructional time under a block schedule, the quality of teaching must be improved to provide for more in-depth learning. Most educators seem to agree that the era of the "sage on stage" should be replaced by teaching strategies that more actively involve all learners and more effectively accommodate differing learning styles. Moreover, issues relating to the relevancy of curriculum and the overall learning environment have become paramount. Teachers find that they must deal with a wide range of ability levels in each class period and must work harder than ever to establish positive relationships with students. All of this takes time, and block scheduling provides more opportunities for success. Clarence M. Edwards commented that "if students and teachers worked with fewer classes and fewer people each day, they could focus more time and energy on improving instruction and increasing learning" (Edwards, 1993, p. 78). Clearly, if the extended class period is educationally beneficial, planners must be cautious not to sacrifice this advantage in order to resolve scheduling problems or by making concessions to interest groups.

Benefits of Block Scheduling

There are many benefits claimed for block scheduling. When one examines workshop materials, packets prepared by high schools using block scheduling, and textbooks and articles, the case made in behalf of block scheduling by its proponents becomes very compelling. When enumerated, the list typically includes about 15 positive statements, or improvements, that are attributed to the use of block scheduling in a school. Some of these claims are merely statements of fact, some are based on empirical data, and others are more anecdotal in nature. But all schools that have implemented block scheduling seem to report a positive set of outcomes. Dianne Hampton of the Institute for Educational Development lists 15 such benefits and her list is representative of many others. She includes the following:

- Fewer students per day for teachers
- Decrease in the number of class changes
- Time savings
- Increased planning time for teachers
- Opportunity for teachers to use a variety of instructional approaches
- Opportunity for project work
- Opportunity for teachers to become better acquainted with each student
- Additional opportunities for teachers to help students
- Increased time for team teaching and interdisciplinary planning
- Fewer interruptions in the course of the school day
- Fewer discipline problems
- Higher attendance
- More students on the honor roll
- Less paper work during the course of the week
- More time for at-risk students to work with teacher/project (Hampton, 1997, p. 5)

Robert L. Canady and Michael Rettig (1995), perhaps the leading authorities on block scheduling, list eight benefits of the alternating block and an additional seven that are unique to the accelerated block.

In 1995, I conducted a survey among Texas high schools that were using some form of block scheduling. This research, which was published in *Texas Study of Secondary Education*, included an open-ended question that asked principals to identify the two most significant benefits that they would attribute to block scheduling in their schools. Twenty-one surveys were returned and even though respondents were limited to two answers, they generated 10 advantages of block scheduling, including

- A less hectic and stressful schedule
- More opportunities for students

- More relevant instruction
- Extended lab opportunities
- Fewer discipline problems
- Reduced failures
- Better attendance
- Greater scheduling flexibility
- Reduction in the total number of students and preparations
- Increased student achievement (Lybbert, 1996, p. 20)

Those who have investigated block scheduling know that lists such as the one above will be claimed by almost all schools that have any experience with this type of schedule. Criticisms of block scheduling rarely come from students or teachers who have participated in the change from a traditional to a block schedule, and examples of schools turning back to traditional schedules are not to be found. Let's examine a few of the benefits that consistently recur in discussions of block scheduling.

Block Scheduling and
Better-Quality Instruction

In addition to the necessary attention that school districts give to curriculum, there has been a growing awareness that teaching methods must change in order to involve students more in the learning process. The emphasis has already been changing from passive learning to actively engaged learners. The Center for Applied Research and Educational Improvement (1995a) at the University of Minnesota reported that "research indicates that many methods of instruction are more effective than lecture." Most teachers would probably agree with this assessment, and block scheduling supports techniques such as cooperative learning, extended science lab experiments, use of guest speakers and other community resources, presentations and debates, greater use of computer labs, simulation activities, team and interdisciplinary teaching, hands-on projects, and other high engagement lessons. For us as educators, perhaps the easiest way to identify with the importance of actively engaged learners is to recall those times when a teacher was excited about what happened in class—was the teacher telling about something he or she did, or was the teacher talking about something the students did?

The issue, then, seems to be less about which approach to teaching will better serve all learners and more about the extent to which teachers will change their instructional strategies. The extended time period in block scheduling will do as much as anything to resolve that issue. Teachers will find it very difficult to rely primarily on lecturing for longer periods of time, and those who do will probably find themselves and their students exhausted. Nancy McClaran made the point by explaining that "block scheduling is virtually forcing teachers to flex and stretch their instructional repertoire. As a result, one conjectured, students are more interested in their classes, spend less time in the hallways, and behave better" (McClaran, 1994, p. 1). Although most of us would agree that the amount of available time will influence lesson plans, my experience as a principal is that the vast majority of teachers do not need to be "forced" into change. Teachers are constantly searching for new and better ways to improve instruction, and teacher attendance at professional conferences and workshops is usually limited only by budgetary considerations. As teachers realize the benefits of varied teaching methods, they will embrace the opportunities afforded them under block scheduling. Having been involved as an administrator in implementing block scheduling at two high schools, my observation is that more than 90% of the teachers have a positive and successful experience when changing from traditional schedules to some form of the block. Surveys taken in high schools all across the country yield similar conclusions when assessing both student and teacher attitudes in schools that have implemented block scheduling; it is a very popular reform.

Introducing reforms in a school may even contribute to revitalizing teachers whose methods have become stagnated through the years. As experienced teachers find new and innovative approaches to teaching and interact with teachers successfully employing new strategies, they may well view themselves as better teachers. The Center for Applied Research and Educational Improvement (1995b) reported survey results showing that "teachers in 4-period schools believe that their school schedule allows them to do their job more effectively than do teachers in 7-period schools. The survey of student attitudes found that student attitudes were more positive in the 4-period schools across a number of dimensions." Another factor that should contribute to improved instruction is the increased planning time for teachers in a block schedule. In a six- or seven-period day with 50-minute classes, a teacher customarily has one period for planning purposes. The same is generally true for teachers in a block schedule except the teaching load is three classes and the planning period is 90 minutes in length. The additional 40 minutes or so each day can be used to help develop the new teaching strategies that are so necessary for the effective use of the extended class period. Teachers will use this time well, as Gerald M. Mistretta and Harvey B. Polansky found in their survey of teacher attitudes. "Teachers felt the added planning time made them more effective teachers. Almost all (94 percent) wanted the block to remain as a permanent schedule" (Mistretta & Polansky, 1997, p. 29). Taken together, the incentives to change and improve the quality of classroom instruction provide a compelling reason to abandon the traditional schedule in favor of block scheduling.

Reduced Discipline Problems

The experience of schools that have implemented block scheduling has been to realize a significant reduction in discipline problems. Part of the explanation for this is fairly obvious: When you reduce the number of passing periods, you reduce the number of opportunities for disruptions in the hall. Principals try to make a practice of standing in the halls and having teachers stand in the halls during passing periods because of the need to supervise students moving about in close quarters. Most fights at school occur when there is a lack of direct supervision, such as before and after school, passing periods, and during lunch. Tardies will also be reduced for the same reason: Students have fewer chances to be tardy.

The real benefit in terms of school discipline, however, seems to be related to changing the overall school environment. It should not be surprising when both students and teachers report they are happier in a blocked schedule that disciplinary problems decline. The fact that students do better in their classes also affects attendance, failure rates, and other factors that are known to be associated with students who are continuously in trouble at school. As students experience more engagement and success at school, their discipline problems will usually decline dramatically. Dianne Hampton's research revealed that, when a school implements block scheduling, "the number of discipline referrals to the office is reduced by 25-35 percent" (Hampton, 1997, p. 20). In some cases, the results have been even better. Principal Abe Ramirez of Bel Air High School in Ysleta, Texas, reported that "disciplinary referrals have dropped drastically. In one 7-day period, only one referral was logged for 2,000 students. As a result, the job of the assistant principals has changed" (quoted in McClaran, 1994, p. 6). Though not the primary justification for block scheduling, the decrease in disciplinary problems is a significant advantage, and some schools might want to consider it for this reason alone.

Better Attendance

Schools have consistently reported better attendance after implementing a block scheduling plan. Virtually all schools listing the benefits of block scheduling in their handout pamphlets include improved attendance. Several factors probably contribute to this positive outcome after schools change from traditional schedules. First, as students find the overall learning environment to be less stressful and hectic, the school day becomes a more positive experience. Whether or not the student perceives his or her school day as a positive or negative experience will affect daily attendance. Students may also be motivated by knowing that they will miss more in a block schedule by being absent because each day missed is equivalent to two days under the traditional schedule—there is a strong incentive not to miss and risk falling behind in classes. With a 90-minute conference period, teachers are also better able to make inquiries into student absences, and the increased communication with the home may well be a factor. There are probably many other reasons for better attendance but, for whatever reason, it is clear that schools enjoy an increase in attendance following the implementation of block scheduling.

Student Success

Schools consistently report that the number of students on the honor roll increases after a change to block scheduling. That success may be attributed, in part, to students having to do homework or prepare for tests in four classes rather than six or seven classes a day. Another explanation might be that students become more interested in classes that are no longer primarily conducted in a lecture format. Greater student interest in school, coupled with an organizational structure that encourages more learning, is a good formula for success. Art Shaw, principal at Montwood High School in Texas, described his experience as one in which "achievement has risen while failure rates and dropouts have been reduced. We truly feel that we are doing what's best for our learners" (quoted in Hampton, 1997, p. 21).

School Climate: Stress and Pace

The reduced stress and overall calmer educational environment that seems to be so essentially linked to block scheduling was the leading response to the question concerning positive results experienced by schools in the *Texas Study* survey. Factors already discussed, such as fewer passing periods and longer planning periods for teachers, are important in countering what is sometimes referred to as the "frenzied" pace of most high schools.

One change that takes place with block scheduling that teachers certainly respond favorably to is the reduction in the number of students and in the number of different class preparations each day. In an alternating (A/B) block, the total number of class preparations and students during the two days of the entire eight-period schedule may not result in any overall reductions in students or class preparations because the teacher will still have a total of six classes, much like a traditional schedule. However, the teacher will only have half that load on any given day, as well as an extended planning period each day. The accelerated (4 × 4) block will have an even more profound impact on the teacher's daily assignment. Because classes meet every day to allow the completion of a yearlong course in only one semester, the teacher's load is only three classes each day in the most commonly used form of the accelerated block. The teacher will have a maximum of three preparations each semester even if he or she is teaching three different courses and has a student enrollment in the 60 to 80 range. For teachers who have been trying to instruct well over 100 students a day in the traditional schedule this change should make a meaningful difference in their ability to be more effective in the classroom.

Student/Teacher Interactions

It has become increasingly important for teachers to build rapport with their students. Although professionalism, competency, and enthusiasm are at the top of most principals' lists for good teachers, it cannot be denied that teachers are expected to assume more and more responsibility for nurturing individual students and contributing to a positive school environment. Teachers who lack interpersonal skills and fail to invest time in developing relationships also tend to have difficulty in reaching their teaching objectives. We have often heard this problem characterized as "they won't care how much you know until they know how much you care."

One of the benefits of block scheduling is that it provides a real opportunity for teachers to get to know their students better. If the extended period is properly used, it will necessarily involve the teacher working closely with students in groups and with projects. Individual attention should be enhanced. Social studies teacher Monroe Brett, after teaching in a block schedule, made the comment that "improvement in student-teacher relationships is far greater than I expected. My ability to understand each student increased by a factor greater than just doubling classroom time" (Brett, 1996, p. 37). As difficult as it might be to try to quantify an advantage such as improved relationships, it is significant that schools that have implemented block scheduling report so many positive outcomes relating to learning environment issues.

As we examine some of the variations of block schedules, we will find that there are some additional benefits that are unique to the different types of schedules. A final question that must be addressed is how block scheduling affects student achievement as measured by standardized instruments rather than grades or other campus indicators of student success. Because the achievement issue has become contested, it will be considered separately when the criticisms of block scheduling are reviewed.

References

Brett, M. (1996, September). Teaching block-scheduled class periods: A unique educational opportunity. *The Education Digest,* p. 37.

Canady, R. L., & Rettig, M. D. (1995). *Block scheduling: A catalyst for change in high schools.* Princeton, NJ: Eye on Education.

Center for Applied Research and Educational Improvement. (1995a). *Block scheduling questions and answers.* University of Minnesota. (World Wide Web: http://www.coled.umn.edu/CAREIwww/blockscheduling/Q&A/g&a.htm)

Center for Applied Research and Educational Improvement. (1995b). *Report study of the four-period schedule for Amoka-Hennepin District No. 11.* University of Minnesota. (World Wide Web: http://www.coled.umn.edu/CAREIwwwBlockScheduling/Research/REPORTs.HTM)

Edwards, C. M., Jr. (1993, May). Restructuring to improve student performance. *NASSP Bulletin,* p. 78.

Hampton, D. (1997). *Strengthening your block schedule program: Practical teaching strategies for extended class periods.* Medina, WA: Institute for Educational Development.

Lybbert, B. (1996, Fall). Block scheduling: Considerations for adoption and implementation. *Texas Study of Secondary Education,* p. 20.

McClaran, N. (1994, April). Re-examining curriculum. *Texas Association for Curriculum and Development,* p. 1.

Mistretta, G. M., & Polansky, H. B. (1997, December). Prisoners of time: Implementing block schedule in the high school. *NASSP Bulletin,* p. 29.

Suggested Reading

Breaking ranks for high school reform. (1996, October). *The Education Digest,* pp. 4-9.

Burton, T. (1995). *Blocking scheduling: One school's method for success.* AFT Group. (World Wide Web: http://tigerchuh.cleveland-heights.k12.oh.us/Learning/Block/TexasMS.html)

Cawelti, G. (1993, Summer). Restructuring large high schools to personalize learning for all. *ERS Spectrum,* pp. 20-21.

Glasser, W. (1990). *The quality school.* New York: Harper & Row.

Rettig, M. D., & Canady, R. L. (1997, February). All around the block. *The Education Digest,* p. 31.

Shortt, T. L., & Thayer, Y. V. (1997, December). A vision for block scheduling: Where are we now? Where are we going? *NASSP Bulletin,* p. 11.

⊞ 3 ⊞

The Alternating (A/B) Block

The alternating block shown in Table 3.1 has been the most popular form of block scheduling until recently. One explanation for its acceptance as a restructuring mechanism over other models is because of its simplicity and also its similarity in some ways to the traditional schedule it was to replace. An alternating block schedule typically just spreads the existing seven-period schedule over two days, adds an eighth class, and then doubles the class time to 90 minutes per period. The alternating block schedule "feels" much like the traditional schedule—students start out in period one and end in period eight, even though they attend periods one through four on one day and periods five through eight the next day.

The alternating block schedule is usually referred to as an A/B block because most schools designate the starting day under the schedule as the "A" day and follow with the "B" day classes, and then continue to alternate these days throughout the semester. Some schools have elected to use other designations for their days, such as school colors, and they find it appealing to use, say, "green" day and "gold" day.

Class scheduling under an alternating block schedule will be very similar to that of a traditional model. Principals will need to plan on additional electives to accommodate the increased number of periods that have been created—remember, students will now be

TABLE 3.1   Typical A/B Block

A Day	B Day
Period 1	Period 5
Period 2	Period 6
Period 3	Period 7
Period 4	Period 8

180-Day School Year

able to earn eight credits a year. A typical first-year schedule for a freshman student might look like Table 3.2.

Some of the classes in this freshman schedule—such as physical education, speech, and keyboarding—will be one-semester courses in many districts. As students complete these one-semester courses, there will be a need for other one-semester courses or electives to be positioned on the schedule to absorb these students at midyear. Although this has always presented a problem for schedulers, it is exacerbated by an increase to eight in the total number of class periods under the A/B plan. Table 3.2 also illustrates another concern that schedulers must consider. It is very desirable to try to balance the student's class load as much as possible by not having too many difficult classes on either the "A" or the "B" day. Too many core academic, or honors, courses on one day could mitigate some of the benefits attributed to block scheduling. If a student has weak academic skills, an unbalanced schedule may even result in excessive absences on the day the student is overloaded with difficult classes.

As administrators work on implementing the alternating block schedule in their schools, several other problems unique to the A/B plan may arise. For example, teacher's conference periods can no longer be moved anywhere in the schedule as attempts are made to change class sections or when adding or dropping courses. A teacher's conference period may still be moved around within the "A" or "B" schedule, but care must be exercised not to have the two conference periods on one day and four teaching assignments on the other day. When using a computerized scheduling program, this should be one of the restrictions programmed. When scheduling by hand, or hand scheduling whatever percent of conflicts the computer could not resolve, separate the "A" and "B" days, even if only with a red line drawn down the paper as a reminder.

TABLE 3.2   Typical A/B Sample Block With Times and Freshman
Schedule (8 Credits)

	A Day (Green Day)	B Day (Gold Day)	
8:00 - 9:30	English I	Physical Science	(90 Minutes)
9:35 - 11:15	Spanish I	Algebra I	(100 Minutes-10 Extra for Homeroom)
11:20 -12:05	Lunch	Lunch	(45 Minutes)
12:10 - 1:40	Keyboarding	Speech I	(90 Minutes)
1:45 - 3:15	Phys. Edu.	World History	(90 Minutes)

Typical "Year-Long" Course of English I - 90 Days X 90 Min. = 8,100 Min.

Balancing the teacher's class assignments should also be a priority while working on the master schedule. Teachers should be con-
sulted concerning their preferences and any aspects of their assignments that might be uniquely affected by an alternating block
schedule. Science teachers, for example, will probably want to have
classes that have the same lab requirements on the same day. Some
teachers will prefer having the same preparations on the same day
and others will prefer to have some variety in their teaching day.
Involving teachers in these decisions will help them buy into the new
schedule, and the transition to block scheduling should be smoother.
The degree of difficulty in scheduling teacher's preferences will, of
course, depend on the size of the faculty and the number of sections
of each class. Priority, however, should be given to balancing the
overall schedule to serve the needs of the students.

Double Blocking

One option that administrators have under the A/B plan is to
determine that some classes need to meet each day and then schedule them accordingly. Double blocking a class simply means that it
meets each day, which has the effect of providing that class with
twice the time available for those meeting every other day. The double-blocked class must be on corresponding periods across the
schedule, such as the first class period classes on both "A" and "B"

days (actually periods one and five). Many teachers, particularly in activities and athletics, will feel they must meet with their students every day in order to satisfy the demands of specialized classes. In fact, this is rarely the case, and yearbook sponsors will find they can meet deadlines and coaches will find they can field competitive teams meeting every other day. In most schools, however, coaches of major sports tend to be able to persuade decision makers into making this concession. A result of this type of scheduling may be to severely limit athletes in their academic class choices because students double blocked in one program for 4 years will find that they have invested 25% of their high school career in that one activity. As we will see later, better solutions are available.

A more appropriate use of double blocking could be developed around trying to reach an educational objective that fulfills a student's academic needs or that remediates deficiencies. For example, many states and local districts will have a 2-year extended algebra class available in order to give students with a weak math background twice the seat time in which to achieve content mastery. A double-blocked extended algebra class will allow the student to have the additional needed instructional time while keeping the student on pace with his or her peers. Another beneficial use of double blocking is in developing and supporting work-cooperative programs. Such programs, usually limited to juniors and seniors, generally are designed with a vocational class meeting at one time period and a supervised early release from school to work in a related job field. This release time can be considered as double blocked time and students can obtain additional credits while learning on the job. Vocational and technical training programs have begun to enjoy a resurgence as schools try to promote "real world" authentic learning opportunities. Double blocking should be used sparingly because it reduces the total number of classes the student is taking to seven— six regular 90-minute periods and one double-blocked period meeting each day.

A/B Variations

We have examined building the A/B block around an eight-period class schedule over two days, but some schools have adjusted their schedules in order to have a seven-period schedule. The seven-period day is accomplished by having three regular 90-minute periods and then one shorter period, slotted to meet daily. This daily period is usually positioned at the beginning or end of the day to support athletics or activities, although it could be anywhere in the schedule. A similar variation would be to keep the four extended periods and add a shorter daily period that would constitute a ninth period. The daily period is always shorter in length, and the actual number of minutes may well result from predetermined beginning and ending times for schools.

The schedule represented in Table 3.3 would provide for six extended class periods of 95 minutes each and one 55-minute class period that would meet every day. The 55-minute period is certainly long enough to provide some options in scheduling specialized programs. If any academic classes are designated for the 55-minute daily class, they should be carefully chosen and probably limited to single sections of regular classes and electives. Remember, if a teacher is teaching the same course in a 95-minute class and again in a 55-minute class the teacher has two very different preparations.

The schedule shown in Table 3.4 might prove attractive to a number of schools. It allows extended periods while providing a daily class period that would meet each day at the end of the day. If the last period, period nine, is used exclusively for elective activity classes and athletics, it would allow for dismissal from school for other students at 2:40 p.m. Regular academic classes should not be scheduled into this daily time slot.

Scheduling Considerations

As decisions are made in structuring the format of the alternating block schedule, some other potential problems should be considered. Care should be taken not to try to build too much into the school day. If, for example, planners agreed to the above schedule creating nine classes for some students and then added a homeroom period as well, the advantage of a less hectic atmosphere in school might well be diminished. Indeed, even with a simple eight-period configuration some students and teachers will find the pace of school demanding even though the schedule is spread over 2 days. Some have suggested that these inherent problems with the alternating block schedule make it more appropriate as a beginning step in re-

TABLE 3.3.   7 Periods of 95-Minute Classes, 2 Lunch Shifts

Period 1/4	8:15 - 9:50	95-minute class
Period 2/5	9:55 - 11:35	100 minutes (extra 5 for announcements)
Period 3/6 - Lunch	11:40 - 12:20	1st lunch - 40 minutes
	12:30 - 1:10	2nd lunch - 40 minutes
	12:25 - 2:00	95-minute class time for 1st lunch students
	11:40 - 12:30	95-minute split class time for 2nd lunch
	1:15 - 2:00	students
Period 7	2:05 - 3:00	55-minute class (every day)

structuring and that this type of schedule might best be used as a transitional step to the accelerated block.

A few logistical matters that may help principals avoid some problems unique to the A/B plan should be reviewed. Attendance policies should be examined and issues resolved prior to implementing the block, and students and parents need to be informed about implications of absences with a block schedule. First, any absence becomes more significant because it represents lost instructional time comparable to 2 missed days with a traditional schedule. Under the alternating block schedule, however, missed school days should be viewed independently as "A" or "B" day absences. If state or local policy sets a maximum number of allowed absences (say 10, for example) before severe sanctions are applied, it must be understood that this means a student can only miss 5 "A" days or 5 "B" days. In a 90-day semester, a class in an alternating block schedule will only meet 45 times, and students can develop attendance problems quickly if administrators do not monitor a student's specific "A" and "B" day absences carefully.

The related issue of unavoidable student absences for doctor/ dental appointments, athletic contests, field trips, and other school programs should be addressed early. Administrators should predetermine the "A" and "B" days at the beginning of the year and mark them on the school calendar, and any missed days due to weather should be made up on scheduled make-up days or at the end of the year. By organizing the year in advance, the principal will be able to advise a parent on scheduling long-term regular orthodontic appointments, for example, in a manner that will spread the absences between the alternating days. Principals will also easily be able to keep a running total of the number of "A" or "B" days already dis-

TABLE 3.4   8 Periods of 85-Minute Classes, 1 45-Minute Class, 1
              Lunch Shift

Period 1/5	8:00 - 9:25	85-minute class
Period 2/6	9:30 - 11:00	90-minutes (extra 5 for announcements)
Period 3/7	11:05 - 12:30	85-minute class
Lunch	12:35 - 1:10	35-minute lunch
Period 4/8	1:15 - 2:40	85-minute class
P-9 (every day)	2:45 - 3:30	45-minute class

rupted for field trips and programs. In a block schedule, principals
must be diligent on attendance issues.

Administrators will want to devise a method to clearly communicate to both students and teachers which day the school is on each
morning. While not a major concern, it does help avoid the repeated
"is this an A or B day?" question at the start of each school day. Most
schools have posters with "A" or "B" or other designations printed
on them and display these at the office or some other central location
each morning. Other schools rely on electronic signboards, postings
at teachers' doors, or other such devices.

Suggested Reading

Burton, T. (1995). *Blocking scheduling: One school's method for success. AFT Group.* (World Wide Web: http://tigerchuh.cleveland-
heights.k12.oh.us/Learning/Block/TexasMS.html)
Miller, E. (1992, March-April). Breaking the tyranny of the schedule.
The Harvard Educational Letter, pp. 6-8.

⊞ 4 ⊞

The Accelerated (4 × 4) Block

The accelerated block schedule, also referred to as the 4 × 4 plan, has been gaining acceptance at a rapid pace. When the current restructuring movement began to incorporate block scheduling as a basic component of change, the alternating schedule was initially more popular due to both the advantages it offered and its similarity to the existing traditional schedule. As reformers have had more time to reflect on the relative merits of the various types of block scheduling and much more information has become available, the accelerated block schedule has become the model of choice. In Virginia, for example, the number of high schools on the 4 × 4 plan has already surpassed the number of A/B schools.

The accelerated block schedule represents a real departure from the traditional schedule. Typically, the 4 × 4 approach is organized around four 90-minute classes that are repeated every day until the end of the semester. What has normally been thought of as a full year course will be completed in a semester and a one-half credit course will be completed at the mid-point of the semester.

The accelerated block schedule represented in Table 4.1 enjoys almost all of the general benefits of block scheduling, such as decreased discipline problems, better attendance, and improvements in student academic success. Claims of improved instructional pedagogy are even more compelling as teachers have fewer class prepa-

TABLE 4.1   Typical 4 × 4 Block

1st Semester (90 Days)		2nd Semester (90 Days)	
Period 1	Period 1	Period 1	Period 1
Period 2	Period 2	Period 2	Period 2
Period 3	Period 3	Period 3	Period 3
Period 4	Period 4	Period 4	Period 4
45 Days	45 Days	45 Days	45 Days

rations each semester. Students are able to profit from opportunities to earn 32 credits based on four classes each semester.

The freshman schedule shown in Table 4.2 would be representative of what a student might expect in the first year in high school. Note that one-semester courses such as speech and health would last for a period of about 45 days. Schools on the accelerated block schedule will, in effect, redefine their school year into four terms in order to facilitate the semester classes. Consideration should be given to grade reporting periods because the semester will no longer align with traditional 6-week grading periods. Administrators will probably want to have a grade reporting date halfway through the first term, or at about 22 days into the semester, and again at the mid-point of the semester. Such an approach will yield eight grade reporting periods in the course of a school year.

Unique 4 × 4 Benefits

In addition to the benefits already discussed, the accelerated block schedule has some unique features. Implementation of the 4 × 4 plan will immediately reduce the teachers' student loads to half of that in an alternating block and significantly less than the traditional schedule. With only three classes, teachers can reasonably anticipate total enrollment of about 75 students each semester. As a related advantage, because the classes are divided by semester and only half the students will be in those classes at any one time, the number of textbooks needed will be cut in half.

Just as teachers will have fewer classes, students will also benefit from having to prepare for only four classes each semester. Students should find that they have much more time to focus on homework,

TABLE 4.2   4 × 4 Sample Block With Times and Freshman
Schedule (8 Credits)

8:30 - 9:30	English I	Physical Science	90 minutes
9:35 - 11:15	Spanish I	Algebra I	100 min. (10 extra for homeroom)
11:20 - 12:05	L u n c h	L u n c h	45 minutes
12:10 - 1:40	Key boarding	Speech Health	90 minutes
1:45 - 3:15	Physical Education	World History	90 minutes

45 Days   45 Days   45 Days   45 Days
(1st Term) (2nd Term) (3rd Term) (4th Term)

Typical "Year-Long" Course of English I - 90 Day X 90 Min. = 8,100

study for tests, and become actively engaged in the learning opportunities in the extended classes. As students enter their senior year, they may have already accumulated as many as 24 credits and may be able to take a reduced class load that will allow for even greater concentration in course work. Some seniors will find that the increased flexibility of block scheduling will allow them to be involved in work cooperatives or other specialized programs. Other students will find that the expansive schedule of classes available to them will allow them to take on academic challenges such as Advanced Placement (AP) courses or concurrent college credit courses. Virtually all schools that implement block scheduling realize an increased demand for both electives and honors classes.

An important educational benefit of the accelerated block schedule is that it provides opportunities for students who are academically weak to retake first semester failed classes immediately. Typical core classes, such as English, will have only half the students in school enrolled in the spring semester, and a student would be able to enroll again for English in the fall semester if he or she has failed the class. Students who make every effort to repeat classes immediately will have profited from having just had the class, and they should be able to remain on pace with their peer group. Because so many extra credits (32) are built into the block schedule, there is no real disadvantage in taking the class again in the spring semester, and keeping students from falling behind is educationally very desirable. Indeed, the prospect of taking new classes and having new teachers at midyear can contribute to heightened student interest in academics. In a study of student attitudes working in the 4 × 4 plan,

J. Casey Hurley found that "students reported they liked the new schedule because they were getting better grades, they had more time for in-depth study, they received more individual attention from teachers, their lives were less hectic, and they had a fresh start after the semester" (Hurley, 1997, p. 65).

Unique Problems Associated
With the Accelerated Block

Because the accelerated block schedule not only includes extended class periods but also reorganizes the time frame for completion of classes, it has created concern about several issues that are impacted by this new schedule.

Staffing Increases

The necessary process of developing new electives and other classes also raises the difficult issue of additional staffing. Personnel costs remain the largest item in school budgets and planners may find that their staffing needs are in conflict with limited financial resources. Though this is a problem for any form of block scheduling that increases the total number of credits, it seems to be more pronounced in the 4 × 4 plan. In some instances, it may prove necessary to delay, or phase-in some of the enrichment classes. It may be possible to employ part-time professionals to teach one or two specialized courses. For example, a nurse might be hired to teach one class of home health care or an introductory nursing course. State guidelines will frequently allow noncertified professionals to teacher courses that are vocationally or technically aligned with school curriculum. The staffing needs to fully implement block scheduling must be considered early in the discussions relative to committing to plan. Stakeholders must be willing to undertake some additional costs for both personnel and staff development.

Sequencing/Retention

One of the criticisms frequently leveled at the 4 × 4 plan is that scheduling may result in circumstances in which there will be significant time gaps between courses that teachers contend should be taught in uninterrupted sequence. The case is usually made in reference to foreign language and math classes. The worst-case scenario finds a student taking Spanish 1, for example, in the fall and completing that course by the end of the semester. Due to scheduling problems, the student does not take the follow-up course of Spanish 2 until the spring semester of the next year, resulting in a 1-year gap between two courses that are usually taught consecutively. Critics assert that the student will not be able to retain the knowledge base necessary to be successful in the Spanish 2 course. Although the situation described is obviously a concern, two factors mitigate the possibility of the problem becoming significantly detrimental to the student. First, the parameters of the problem can almost certainly be changed with careful scheduling. Students might be required to take the follow-up course in the second semester and then take the next two levels of the subject the following year, in this case Spanish 3 and 4. Although workable, this solution may result in an overly rigid schedule or one in which students complete their foreign language well in advance of graduation, recreating the retention issue as it relates to high school and college.

A better approach would be to make certain that students have a maximum gap of one semester between courses in which it is believed that retention will become a barrier to successful learning. A second consideration is to question the real impact delays will have on retention. To some extent, it seems unreasonable for educators to view a gap in sequence with so much concern; we are often confronted with students taking courses after extensive delays, or transfers having to take classes out of the school's normal sequence. Moreover, because an important justification for longer periods is the belief in a better quality of in-depth learning, it might well be that students will retain the learning for a longer period of time. Dianne Hampton claimed that "material is taught more thoroughly in longer blocks. Discussions, application to real life situations, and a deeper understanding of the content is evident in the extended class. Therefore, students retain the learned material and transition to the next level of the content is smooth" (Hampton, 1997, p. 20). The amount of material the student fails to retain may well be more closely linked to the quality of the initial learning than to any arbitrary timelines. Michael Rettig and Robert Canady reported that "experienced teachers from 4 × 4 schools say they can discern little educational significance between the difference in retention of students

who recently completed a prerequisite and other students with greater time lapses between courses" (Rettig & Canady, 1997, p. 31).

Overall, the concerns about retention in an accelerated block schedule do not appear to be justified.

Yearlong Activities/Athletics

Opposition to the adoption of an accelerated block schedule may initially come from fine arts teachers and athletic coaches—an interesting coalition. Teachers who direct plays, conduct music programs, and sponsor yearbooks and newspapers are among those who frequently view the 4 × 4 plan as a threat to their programs. These concerns seem to be somewhat valid; some schools that have implemented the accelerated block schedule have experienced diminished enrollment in fine arts activity programs, particularly music. If students are enrolled only in the fall or spring semester, it will be very difficult to maintain a competition quality band, drama, or debate program.

One possible solution to the problem of limiting traditionally yearlong activities would be to modify the 4 × 4 block by building in alternating classes restricted to these programs. To avoid other potential conflicts, it might be best to position these A/B classes either at the first or last time period on the opposite end of the schedule from athletics. Such an alternating period, however, could be placed anywhere in the schedule with little effect on the overall scheme other than adding a period to the student's schedule and increasing the class load to five (from four in the standard 4 × 4 configuration). A variation allowing the classes to actually meet every day as well as all year long would be to split the 90-minute period, creating two classes of about 45 minutes each, which would, again, increase the student's load to five classes. Students would attend a class—band for example—for the first 45 minutes and then be dismissed to another elective, such as art, drama, newspaper and yearbook, or even another music class, such as choir, jazz band, or even music history. If a student were involved only in the class meeting the second half of the 90-minute period and that period was the first of the day, then the student might be allowed to arrive at school just prior to the time scheduled for that class. Consideration for the needs of the students involved in cocurricular programs coupled with careful scheduling should allow administrators to resolve most of the potential objections from fine arts teachers and activity directors. Another option is, of course, just to allow the class to meet all year long, even though this would result in some students earning two credits each year they are involved in the program and also monopolizing 25% of their high school graduation plan.

Athletics can pose similar challenges unless the sports program is an after school activity, as it is in many districts. If, however, the athletics period is a part of the regular day, usually meeting first or last period, coaches will insist that they must have their players in class each day as well as at practices. Several possible modifications to the standard accelerated block schedule might help administrators accommodate the athletics program. First, the semesters should be viewed in terms of fall and spring sports as some students will only play football or baseball. A student might well be involved in athletics each day in the fall and then be in another class or program in the spring. Students wanting to play both fall and spring sports will be committing a disproportionate share of their time to one activity in a standard accelerated block schedule. A better solution might be to have the regularly scheduled 90-minute classes end by approximately 2:30 p.m. and have athletics for the next 45 minutes and after school for practices. Other activities classes or even remediation could be scheduled at this time, although planners must realize that any additional class scheduling will increase staffing needs as well as create conflicts if any single section activity class occurs at the same time as the athletics period.

Advanced Placement Classes

Advanced Placement (AP) classes have become increasingly popular as high schools have attempted to provide challenging courses for college-bound students. The AP course is designed to allow students to take an exit examination at the end of the course. If the score is high enough, most colleges and universities will grant credit on the college transcript. The AP tests are given in several different subject areas, and schools offering the AP courses develop them around specially trained teachers, enrichment materials, and a rigorous curriculum.

Because the AP exams are given in May, students completing fall AP courses are believed to be at a disadvantage due to the gap of almost five months between the end of the course and the testing date. There is a legitimate concern that any loss of retention or lack of study opportunities will adversely affect student performance. If administrators schedule all AP courses in the spring, it can unbalance the overall schedule, create direct conflicts between AP and other courses, and overload the student with too many difficult classes in the same semester.

Several possible adjustments would help minimize or eliminate these concerns. One solution would be to use an alternating block schedule for most of the AP classes, although some could still be scheduled on the regular 4 × 4 plan in the spring semester. Organized as A/B classes, the student would attend his or her AP English class on "A" days and an AP science class on the "B" days, for example. This arrangement would allow the student to benefit from the extended class periods and yet have a yearlong course that would support preparation for the AP exams. Scheduling would be much like that already described for accommodating fine arts classes and, indeed, the AP course might be built into a first or last class period time slot. This would allow a student to enroll in only one of the available AP courses and, on the alternating day, either to arrive late or leave early, depending on the schedule. It should be noted, however, that this would result in the student being enrolled in three regular 4 × 4 plan classes and two alternating classes for a total of five classes in a semester, even though the yearly credit total would still be eight. Staffing problems would also emerge, as this scheme effectively creates a half-teaching assignment for one time slot that could only be balanced with another alternating class or a duty assignment.

Another design to address the AP exam problem would be to structure a shorter class period that meets each day in addition to the existing 90-minute classes. Just as in the alternating block model, such a time period can prove beneficial for some classes such as AP courses, activities, or athletics. Even scheduling one or two AP courses in this shortened period at the beginning or the end of school, combined with some AP courses scheduled in the spring, might create a schedule that would provide for the needs of most students. A different organizational approach using shorter periods than the accelerated block is designed around would be to schedule two AP courses into the same time slot and split the time within the period. Such a class would need to be team taught in most cases and could provide a real opportunity for interdisciplinary instruction, as the two AP courses run all year long and culminate with the AP exams and two credits.

Some schools using the accelerated block schedule have chosen to keep AP courses balanced in both the fall and spring semesters and follow up with study and review sessions in the spring for those students who took the course work in the fall. As most schools already provide some form of tutoring for students taking mastery tests, SAT and ACT exams, or other standardized tests, administrators should be able to develop a tutorial support system that will assist students needing to review for AP exams.

Finally, the issue of students being at a disadvantage because of poor retention should be carefully examined. Although some schools have reported lower AP scores in a standard unmodified 4×4 plan, just as many schools have reported that there was no adverse impact for first-semester AP students. Some schools have claimed the scores have improved for students in both semesters. If, in fact, students in extended classes learn material in more depth, then retention problems should be minimal and scoring differences insignificant, or attributable to other factors.

4×4 Variations

We have already addressed some modifications that can take place within the standard four-period day that do not affect the structure of the schedule, such as alternate blocking of two classes at one time period, or even splitting class time between two classes and giving each class approximately 45 minutes. Planners should, however, view the schedule as a tool to be manipulated to achieve goals considered important by stakeholders in the school community.

The schedule outlined in Table 4.3 would provide for a relatively standard accelerated block schedule while including a 45-minute daily period before school that could be offered as an optional class for students. Such a class period could involve electives such as band, or it might be used as the athletics period. This schedule could just as easily have the daily period at the end of the day, or even be positioned at another time slot.

TABLE 4.3   Four Periods of 85 Minutes

Early/Zero Period	7:45 - 8:30	45-minute class
Period 1	8:35 - 10:00	85-minute class
Period 2	10:05 - 11:35	90-minute (5 extra for announcements)
Lunch	11:40 - 12:20	40-minute lunch
Period 3	12:25 - 1:50	85-minute class
Period 4	1:55 - 3:20	85-minute class

Many possible variations of the 4 × 4 plan are possible. If anything, principals may need to stress keeping the schedule somewhat simple the first year of implementation rather than trying to satisfy every perceived problem or special interest. Remember, at the core of block scheduling is the belief that the extended period will result in a better quality education and short, or split, periods may well function contrary to that principle. Some variations and even concessions will be necessary, but proceed with caution.

References

Hampton, D. (1997). *Strengthening your block schedule program: Practical teaching strategies for extended class periods.* Medina, WA: Institute for Educational Development.

Hurley, J. C. (1997, December). The 4 × 4 block scheduling model: What do students have to say about it? *NASSP Bulletin*, p. 65.

Rettig, M. D., & Canady, R. L. (1997, February). All around the block. *The Education Digest*, p. 31.

Suggested Reading

Hinn, D. M. (1996, April 12). *VMEA block scheduling statement.* Virginia Music Education Association. (World Wide Web: http://www.music.vt.edu/notes/1990years/1996/no1/block.html)

Mississippi Department of Education. (1996, April). *Final report on modular/block scheduling presented to the Mississippi Board of Education.* (World Wide Web: http://www2.msstate.edu//anell/modular.html)

Rettig, M. D. (1997, September 1). *Directory of high school scheduling models in Virginia 1997-98.* James Madison University. (World Wide Web: http://www.jmu.edu/edleadership/chart972.htm)

⊞ **5** ⊞

Modified Blocks, Trimesters, and Other Alternative Schedules

As each school decision-making team, or committee, evaluates the merits of reorganizing the day around a new scheduling format, it should carefully consider student needs, problems, and goals, and develop a schedule that offers real solutions. Though many schools have experienced success with a standard alternating or accelerated block schedule, the movement to site-based leadership has empowered decision makers with a great deal of freedom to innovate and experiment.

Trimester Plan

The trimester plan incorporates both extended class periods and unique timelines into a schedule that is fundamentally different from either the block schedule or the traditional schedule. Whereas the standard alternating block retains yearlong courses and the standard accelerated block covers a yearlong course in one semester, a trimester schedule provides for the completion of a yearlong class in two thirds of a school year.

The configuration illustrated in Table 5.1 is based on five 75-minute classes that meet each day. Other trimester models could be

TABLE 5.1   Standard Trimester Plan

60 Days (1st Term)	60 Days (2nd Term)	60 Days (3rd Term)
Period 1	Period 1	Period 1
Period 2	Period 2	Period 2
Period 3	Period 3	Period 3
Period 4	Period 4	Period 4
Period 5	Period 5	Period 5

built around four classes of longer duration, six classes of shorter duration, or any other number of possible modifications. The trimester has proven a popular alternative for some schools as it represents a less radical departure from the traditional schedule than does the typical block format when viewed from the standpoint of the daily schedule.

When the trimester schedule is viewed in terms of the yearly number of course sections and semesters, it represents a new approach to restructuring. A student's schedule in a five-period trimester plan is represented by the sample shown in Table 5.2.

Proponents of the trimester schedule contend that reallocating time in this manner will accrue essentially all of the benefits attributed to block scheduling. Trimester schools report better attendance, fewer disciplinary problems, improved academic success, a better educational environment, more quality teaching and learning time, and so forth. Just as it is difficult to quantify subjective indicators of improvement or to establish clear causal links between block scheduling and objective indicators of improvement, it is probably even more difficult to make undisputed claims about a plan that is something of a compromise between traditional and alternative models. We might question how significant the differences are between a schedule that represents a transition from six 55-minute classes in a traditional schedule to five 75-minute classes in a trimester. Or, how much will the instructional pedagogy really change if the extended period is only 20 minutes longer? If, however, the change is from seven 45-minute classes to five 75-minute classes, have we now passed a meaningful threshold that will substantially alter the dynamics of the school day? It would be very difficult to isolate the true nexus of change and all its attendant benefits.

TABLE 5.2   Typical Trimester Sample With Times and Freshman Schedule: 7½ Credits

8:00 - 9:15	English I	English I	Speech	75 minutes
9:20 - 10:45	Health	World History	World History	85 min. (10 extra for homeroom)
10:50 - 12:05	Algebra I	Algebra I	Algebra (extend)	75 minutes
12:10 - 12:55	Lunch	Lunch	Lunch	45 minutes
1:00 - 2:15	Phys. Science	Phys. Science	Journalism	75 minutes
2:20 - 3:35	Physical Ed.	Spanish I	Spanish I	75 minutes
	60 Days	60 Days	60 Days	

Typical "Year-Long" Course of English I - 120 Days X 75 Min. = 9,000 Minutes

Trimester Advantages

The trimester may result in a school's realizing most of the advantages of block scheduling as well as some unique to the trimester plan. Certainly, implementing a trimester should increase the possibility of a smooth transition from the traditional schedule because the change is not as pronounced in any single term as is the change to a 90-minute block schedule plan. Teachers who are adapting lesson plans may be able to incorporate cooperative learning and other strategies by merely adding another activity segment to the day's lesson. Teachers should certainly gain from having fewer students than they had with the traditional schedule. A normal teaching assignment in a five-period trimester would include four classes and a conference period. Administrators will also find that the trimester provides a plan that allows each teacher to have as many, or more, overall class sections each year when compared to other models.

One instructional issue that favors the trimester over standard block schedules is the total number of minutes lost or gained under each proposal. The loss of instructional time in the block schedule must be offset by better quality teaching and learning in extended periods of 90 minutes. The 75-minute extended period for a yearlong trimester course (two trimesters, 120 days) will result in 9,000 instructional minutes, the same as was formerly available in a traditional schedule of 50-minute classes in a 180-day school year. The trimester is not as dependent on the "better quality" issue, as is the block schedule as there is no actual loss of time.

Another attractive characteristic of the trimester is that it is very flexible and adaptable, if for no other reason than it provides an additional term in which to plan programs and provide educational options. Similar to the 4 × 4 plan, students who fail one term, although not both, can retake that course in the last term and still be on pace with their peers. This assumes, of course, that the student failed in one of the first two trimesters rather than the last one and that a "trailer" section of that course is available in the last term. A trimester also allows for easy scheduling of half-credit courses and electives and could promote the development of one-term courses that support specific goals. If, for example, a reading class were needed in conjunction with English, the English course could be taught in two of the terms and the reading class in one term. Planners might consider extended arts or math an area of academic need for students at their school and require a full yearlong course of three terms for one and a half credits. Because the trimester plan provides 15 possible courses, there is ample room in the schedule to combine class times in order to facilitate the introduction of work cooperatives, tech prep, or other specialized training programs.

In the schedule shown in Table 5.3, a senior might be working in a tech prep program that would release him or her at midday to receive advanced course work and concurrent college credit in a community college program. The tech prep period illustrated would utilize two of the existing 75-minute periods and would involve no unusual scheduling changes or time adjustments. Other opportunities will exist to add classes that reflect campus and district goals, such as a freshmen study skills program, a community service component, an SAT prep class, or one of many other possibilities that the trimester approach seems flexible enough to accommodate.

Finally, it should be noted that the trimester plan can also allow the same kinds of variations that can be structured into other forms of block scheduling. One of the class periods could be shortened to allow yearlong participation in elective activity classes or athletics. A shortened class period simply could be placed at the beginning or at the end of the day to create a shorter daily first or fifth class while lengthening the other classes by five or ten minutes each. In all likelihood, however, the five-class period, three-term model will be adaptive enough without additional modifications.

TABLE 5.3   Senior Schedule on Modified Trimester

Government		AP English 4		AP English 4
Trigonometry		Calculus		Economics
Music/Band		Music/Band		Science Elective
Tech. Prep.		Tech. Prep.		Tech. Prep.

Trimester Problems

Because the trimester approach includes a third term, scheduling must be done very carefully, and student class needs and course conflicts must be projected over three time periods rather than two. Even so, it will not be possible to provide enough sections of classes in the third term to meet the needs of all students who have failed, except, perhaps, in very large schools. The ability to retake failed courses and stay on pace academically will probably be a hit-and-miss proposition at best. In addition, the very nature of a schedule that includes 15 time slots will result in the need for many new elective classes. Principals at trimester schools indicate that expanding the elective choices is critical to making the plan work.

The concern about a student's ability to retain information after delays in course sequencing has been suggested as a disadvantage to the trimester plan. Just as this criticism was associated with the 4 × 4 plan, some teachers feel strongly that, to maximize student success, courses such as foreign language and math should be taught in uninterrupted increments. The trimester plan creates the possibility that a student might have a course in the first and second trimester terms followed by a gap that might extend until the second and third trimester terms of the next year. AP students could also be at a disadvantage if the AP course is offered in the first two terms and the AP exam is administered in May. Each of these problems, however, can be resolved with careful scheduling or the use of such solutions examined in the accelerated block schedule section.

One problem that is potentially serious is the issue of transfer students. Because the trimester plan segments the school year into thirds, students on both traditional schedules and block schedules will not be able to align their previous school's classes with the timelines in the trimester school when they transfer during the year. If, for example, a student in an alternating block schedule finishes the first half of a yearlong math course and then transfers to a trimester school, he or she will be either approximately two months ahead or behind in the new school. The students may have to sit through material again or struggle to catch up with the class. When viewed in terms of the student's entire academic load, this problem may seriously impact his or her ability to be successful in these classes. The same situation also works in reverse as students from trimester schools transfer to other schools, only to be confronted with very difficult scheduling problems, some of which cannot be resolved. These conflicts may actually result in some students being unable to meet minimum attendance requirements to gain credit in some classes.

As the principal of a high school on an alternating block schedule in a district adjacent to a large trimester high school, I can assure you that it is often impossible to provide transfer students with a workable schedule. Further complicating this issue for those considering the trimester plan is the fact that relatively few schools have implemented trimesters, assuring principals that transfer difficulties will be a continuing problem. Administrators or other decision makers comparing scheduling alternatives in school districts that have large numbers of transient students, such as those near military bases, would probably be well advised to avoid the trimester plan for their schools.

Four-Day Weeks

One innovative approach to reallocating time in the school week is the use of block scheduling for the first 4 days of the week and designating Fridays for other uses. Though a few schools have actually implemented this scheme, most of the organizational designs relative to this concept have been conducted by way of discussions at workshops or among administrators. It is, however, an interesting idea that opens many possibilities for constructively using a significant amount of time each week. The first concern administrators and teachers would have to consider is the additional loss in overall instructional time. This loss of time might be rectified by extending the school calendar a few days or by lengthening the class periods to 105 or 110 minutes.

In the schedule shown in Table 5.4, a full-year course for one credit would have 7,560 minutes of available instructional time as compared to 8,100 in the standard block and about 9,000 in a traditional schedule with 50-minute classes. This represents a significant loss of instructional time if other measures are not taken to remedy the problem.

What advantage would a 4-day school week yield? The absence of regularly scheduled classes on Fridays, or some other day, could be used to provide services to students or services to the professional staff. Some students might be required to attend on Fridays in order to receive tutoring or counseling. Indeed, the "off" day for students might be linked to objective eligibility criteria such as honor roll status, passing standardized tests, or some other such indicators of student academic success. Programs could be designed to help meet the needs of individual students, and the absence of regular classes would ensure adequate staffing to facilitate a wide range of compensatory activities. Administrators might use Friday time to fulfill some disciplinary objective or attendance make-up requirements. Administrators could also use this time to accommodate the many athletic and academic activities that so often cause students to miss class time.

A different use of time made available on Fridays would be to concentrate on in-service programs, curriculum development and alignment, or other planning and restructuring initiatives. In some states, such a change might be particularly warranted if the state curriculum guidelines have undergone significant revisions and teachers need time to become familiar with requirements, to integrate those requirements with their lesson plans and district curriculum alignment strategies, and to network with other professionals. An approach that might result in meeting both student and teacher needs would be to split the time, perhaps having student enrichment activities in the morning and staff development in the afternoon.

Traditional Schedule Modifications

If decision-making teams determine that they are not yet prepared to abandon the traditional schedule but still see benefits to block scheduling, a viable alternative might be to add some extended periods to the existing schedule. One way in which this can

TABLE 5.4   Four-Day Schedule: 105-Minute Block Schedule
Periods

Period 1	8:00 - 9:45
Period 2	9:50 - 11:35
Lunch	11:35 - 12:15
Period 3	12:15 - 2:00
Period 4	2:05 - 3:50

be accomplished is to have some select courses last two class periods, creating a class of approximately 90 minutes within the existing schedule. Students in the 90-minute class would remain in class at the passing period and continue until the end of the next period. The courses selected for these extended periods might include upper level science courses that would benefit from longer lab sessions or classes in which an interdisciplinary team-teaching module is being implemented. A school might have only a few of these extended sections in the schedule and might offer them on an experimental basis.

Administrators should realize that this type of modification to the traditional schedule will probably not result in many of the advantages claimed by schools that are on block scheduling. Any benefits will be limited to those classes utilizing the extended class format, and the teachers in those classes will need to adopt new teaching strategies in order to be successful. An opportunity would exist for these classes to serve as a positive model for other staff members. Extended classes incorporated into a traditional schedule may provide a good first step for change in schools in which a substantial number of teachers are resistant to change.

Five-Period Model

Another compromise effort at restructuring might find schools trying to maintain a schedule similar to the traditional six- or seven-period model while still incorporating extended classes.

Assume that the schedule shown in Table 5.5 represents a significant loss in instructional time because it would almost certainly need

TABLE 5.5   Five Periods of 80-Minute Classes: 10 Credits

Period 1	8:00 - 9:20	80 minutes
Period 2	9:25 - 10:50	85 minutes (5 extra for announcements)
Period 3	10:55 - 12:15	80 minutes
Lunch	12:15 - 12:50	35 minutes
Period 4	12:50 - 2:10	80 minutes
Period 5	2:15 - 3:35	80 minutes

to be formatted with the accelerated block schedule, resulting in 90 days of 80-minute extended periods for a total of 7,200 minutes, or a little over 10% less available time than the standard block schedule. However, with the number of credits increased to a maximum of 40 over 4 years, the opportunities to innovate with specialized courses would be dramatic. For example, students might be required to have five credits in English rather than the usual four, and the additional credit might be taken from English courses such as reading, technical writing, or a number of other possibilities. Graduation requirements would have to be increased, although not necessarily to 40 credits. Increasing the requirement to approximately 30 credits to graduate would provide a good mix: keeping students in school 4 years while allowing juniors and seniors to have a schedule of only four classes. A schedule organized around a five-period day might well realize most of the benefits attributed to block scheduling while still retaining something of the "feel" of the traditional schedule.

Mini-Semesters

Schools have begun to experiment with reallocating blocks of time into a shorter semester, much like the mini-semesters that most colleges offer at various times during the year. The 90-day semester retains a regular schedule of classes, either traditional or blocked, but the semester is only 75 or 80 days in duration. The remaining 10 or 15 days are considered the short term and, similar to the 4-day week, may or may not include all the students. Administrators may work with other stakeholders to designate very specific uses of the mini-semester that are designed to reflect district goals.

TABLE 5.6   80-10 Split With A/B Block Schedule

				10 Days
Period 1	English I	Period 5	French I	Schedule
Period 2	Computer Science	Period 6	Algebra	designed to
Period 3	Art	Period 7	World History	meet specific
Period 4	Biology I	Period 8	Physical Edu.	needs

---------------------- 1st semester - 80 days ----------------

In the 80-day semester illustrated in Table 5.6, there would be a loss of actual instructional time because of both the reduced minutes resulting from block scheduling and the reduced number of days. If, however, the mini-semester were used to remediate academic deficiencies, there might well be a significant advantage to the students with these deficiencies as the entire teaching staff could focus on their needs. Students could expect more intensified instruction as well as more individualized help. This assumes that students in good academic standing did not have to take the mini-course or that they were involved in programs other than the regular instructional schedule. Students who had met a particular standard might be involved in a training program sponsored by industry or participate in another type of school-to-work program in the community. Other enrichment opportunities could be developed to support a wide range of student interests. For example, students in upper level foreign language classes who demonstrate proficiency might be taken on a field trip to another country to further their understanding of both the language and the culture. Or, students might attend a 2-week fine arts or math "camp" conducted by their school or by some other learning institution.

The many variations of block scheduling are so numerous as to confuse planning teams trying to determine which restructuring alternatives are most suited to their students' needs. A hundred teams could design a hundred different ways to reallocate time, and each of them might well have merit. Teams are cautioned, however, to try to have clear goals and objectives in mind and then develop a schedule that will support their students and teachers in successfully reaching those goals.

Suggested Reading

Brown, D., Shatford, B., & Chapman, S. (1997, May). *Trimester evaluation study.* Hurst, TX: Hurst-Euless-Bedford Independent School District.

Canady, R. L., & Rettig, M. D. (1995). *Block scheduling: A catalyst for change in high schools.* Princeton, NJ: Eye on Education.

Lammel, J. (1997). *Where are we now?* Los Angeles County Office of Education: Regions 8 and 11 Professional Development Consortia. (World Wide Web: http://www.acoe.edu/pdc/second/blockscheduling/now.html)

⊞ 6 ⊞

Implementing Block Scheduling

Key Steps

A s block scheduling continues to grow in popularity, it is only a matter of time before interest emerges in your school. The interest may come from newly hired teachers who have been on block schedules in other schools, administrators who have attended conferences or discussed the issue with other administrators, or it may come from another source. Given that some predictions have estimated the number of schools that will adopt block scheduling at more than 80% nationally by the early part of the next century, it is reasonable to assume that at some point your school will undertake an investigation and implementation process. Several key steps should be adhered to so that the potential for success may be maximized.

Plan of Action

A number of important factors should be considered prior to moving forward with any proposals to restructure. Although someone will have to take the lead initially, very soon into developing the plan of action it should be decided which essential stakeholders must be involved in the details of the planning. In some instances, the procedures for important decision making are already codified in local policy or state guidelines. Many campuses are now mandated to engage in shared, or site based, decision making, and these committees typically reflect a cross section of stakeholder interests, such as administrators, teachers, parents, and other community members. Having determined who should be involved, even the plan of action should become the product of a group effort.

The people involved in developing the plan of action will want to consider a number of key decisions that must be made. These decisions, or steps, should be discussed and prioritized. Timelines must be targeted and they must be reasonable. Too many schools have rushed to implement block scheduling without taking the time to build support for the change or involve enough teachers in the process for them to take any ownership of the program. Once adopted, faculty attitudes and support for the change will be the most critical factor in a successful implementation or a bad experiment. Decision makers need to determine what it will take to actually adopt a block scheduling plan. Will the decision be subject to school board approval? What financial resources will be required for staff development? Will more teachers be needed? Finally, the procedure everyone agrees to in order to formalize the decision will be important. Many schools have allowed the faculty to vote on the decision to change to block scheduling as well as the decision on which kind of block scheduling is to be used. If a democratic vote is to be used to make the final choice, it should be understood whether a simple majority or a higher standard will be needed.

Reasons for Change

What is motivating the interest in change? If a change to block scheduling is being contemplated when there is no demonstrated educational need, there probably will not be enough enthusiasm to bring about meaningful change. The committee, or team, studying the proposition should discuss district and campus strategic planning goals and try to determine if block scheduling will significantly contribute to attaining these goals. Student needs and overcoming academic barriers should be the central factor driving the discussions. The committee should consider drop-out rates, the disciplinary climate of the school, attendance, academic achievement, as well as other indicators of effective schools. The information used should be preserved to establish benchmarks necessary to help evaluate block scheduling by measuring improvements.

Research

It is assumed that those who initiated the interest in the reform effort had a basic understanding of block scheduling and its derivatives. The committee providing leadership on the issue must undertake an extensive research effort in order to be fully informed and in a position to answer the many questions that will be asked. Fortunately, a great deal of information is readily available. There are a number of excellent books and articles on the topic, and many of them are referenced for you in this book. One of the best sources of materials is other schools. In some cases, lists of schools using block scheduling and the type of block schedule used are available from state offices or educational organizations. In Texas, for example, the Texas Mentor School Network provides this and other vital information about leading schools. Absent such guidance, an afternoon of phone calling will result in many contacts with schools using block scheduling. Because schools that have implemented block scheduling have had such positive experiences, many of them have already compiled materials into handbooks that outline their process of adopting block scheduling, and in some cases evaluative data such as student and teacher attitudes after two or three years with the new system and other pertinent information. These materials can be extremely valuable as they reflect the actual experience of a school that has already made the transition and the schedule they are using. Another very important source of information is the Internet. Researchers may be surprised to find thousands of sources of information, including studies, schedules, discussions by both proponents and critics, and much more.

After conducting an extensive study of block scheduling, the planning committee will want to gather more information in person and will probably want to start involving more teachers in the process. Schools that have implemented block scheduling have become accustomed to inquiries from other schools and often play host to site visitation teams. Having a group of teachers interact with other teachers in their field can be very persuasive, and it is a relatively inexpensive means to break down barriers to change. Some team members may also be designated to attend conferences and work-shops. In the past several years, almost all statewide administrative conferences in Texas have had at least one break-out session on the various forms of block scheduling. Regional and state educational service centers can also facilitate both the provision of information and workshops. In addition, several groups and individuals conduct seminars, usually one day long, on a commercial basis.

Keeping the Faculty Informed

When the leadership committee reaches the point at which they feel well informed and competent to make recommendations, they should focus on informing and persuading the faculty and, perhaps, other critical interest groups. If site visits have been conducted, some faculty members will already have benefited from this exercise. It is to be hoped that the process has not been secretive anyway, and administrators on the committee have taken advantage of opportunities to share articles and other materials during the previous weeks and months.

Although the committee taking the leadership role on the block scheduling initiative will probably include parents and other community members, it will be necessary to consider whether or not the timing is appropriate for involving the community at large. If community members and students are made to feel that they get to decide the issue, it may be impossible to achieve any kind of consensus for change. There is a normal tendency to resist change, and parents often want to maintain the school structure in the most familiar context. Other parties may feel threatened because of the activities they participate in, rumors they have heard, or other misleading information about block scheduling. Some, like the faculty, will have legitimate questions and concerns. Because the faculty represents the key players who will determine the ultimate success or failure of the reform, they should be the focal point in the process.

Presentations should be made at staff meetings, preferably by the teachers on the committee. Information should be disseminated in a presentation format. It would be wise to present several alternatives, including the alternating block schedule, the accelerated block schedule, modified blocks, and the trimester. Committee members should take the lead in recommending a plan and explaining why it appears superior to the others for your school. Adequate time for questions and discussions must be allowed and the review process should take place over a period of weeks, which will allow teachers ample time to reflect on the choices and to discuss the issues among themselves. This process should culminate with a secret ballot in a vote with a predetermined standard of acceptance. If the faculty decides not to adopt a block scheduling proposal, the principal needs to respect that decision while trying to determine why the effort was rejected. It may be possible to repeat the process again in a year or two with greater sensitivity to the critical issues.

Outside Stakeholders

Even if a decision by the school board is not administratively required to implement block scheduling, the board should be kept well informed. This can be a difficult balancing act for a principal as teachers will feel their professional expertise is not valued if the school board rejects a faculty vote of acceptance. Conversely, the school board members will not want to be in a position in which they feel the decision has already been made and they are merely ratifying that decision. Clearly, the superintendent's role will be crucial in trying to move all stakeholders to a consensus conclusion. Committee members should be prepared to give persuasive presentations to various groups in the community. Handout materials should be prepared that address issues such as the reasons for change, how the plan actually works, the benefits expected, the experiences of other schools, and how block scheduling will affect various sports and activities. Newsletters should be sent out and articles published in local media where practical. Parents and students should be invited to a series of orientation meetings prior to the beginning of the first year of block scheduling.

It is difficult to predict how long such a process might (or should) take, and it will certainly be influenced by the dynamics of the individual schools. A school experiencing excessive disciplinary problems and low academic performance will be more receptive to restructuring than a school that has been successful with a traditional schedule. Administrators will probably want to think in terms of a 1- to 2-year overall process from proposal to implementation.

Case Study: North Charleston High School

The following case study was written by Louis E. Lavely, Jr., chairperson of the Department of Science and athletic director at North Charleston High School in North Charleston, South Carolina.

In the spring of 1993, the faculty and staff of North Charleston High School began to look at several methods to address some of the problems facing the school. These problems included issues that confront every high school, such as high dropout rates, low standardized test scores, and large class size. North Charleston High School also was presented with the unique situation of its third consolidation with another high school in the past 7 years. This consolidation brought several diverse communities together in a facility that was smaller than was needed. After investigation and research to find a solution to this array of challenges, North Charleston High School adopted the A/B form of block scheduling.

The process that North Charleston High School followed in its decision to adopt block scheduling took place in the spring of 1993. The concept of block scheduling was presented to the faculty by the administration, and investigation of this method of scheduling was discussed and reviewed by committees in place through the School Improvement Council. The concerns and questions raised in these meetings were addressed through discussions at the School Improvement Council meetings as well as general faculty meetings.

The next step in the process was to seek input from schools already using the block scheduling format. A committee of about 15 faculty members visited J. L. Mann High School in Greenville, South Carolina, to examine their use of block scheduling. Finally, in a general faculty meeting, consensus was reached that North Charleston High School should proceed in its adoption of the A/B form of block scheduling.

The commitment to begin block scheduling at North Charleston High School meant that several important concerns would have to be addressed. These issues included reservations that were unique to individual academic departments, such as the foreign language department. This department was concerned that students would not receive the necessary drill and practice to master a new language with the block schedule alternating format. The foreign language teachers were unanimous in their desire to teach the same students daily. Though unable to schedule every foreign language class every day, steps were taken by the foreign language department to modify the curriculum and change teaching techniques to meet the demands of block scheduling.

A concern that existed among the entire faculty was how to maintain a student's interest and attention for 90-minute class periods. The consensus was that teaching techniques would have to be altered. Strategies to adjust to block scheduling were discussed and developed within academic departments. In-service training was provided in several areas designed to instruct teachers how to adjust their teaching styles and methods to the longer periods. The teaching technique most relied on was cooperative learning. The entire faculty at North Charleston High School was strongly encouraged to take a cooperative learning course.

Although teachers were concerned with maintaining a student's full attention for 90 minutes, they were also worried that block scheduling would cut their contact time with the students. The A/B block schedule scheme results in a loss of about 30 hours of instructional time per class period per year. This is a result of the alternating nature of this scheduling system. Contact time is 450 minutes during a 2-week period with block scheduling versus 500 minutes of contact time with the traditional schedule during a 2-week period. This loss of contact time was, and still is, very troubling to some teachers. Although there is a loss of class time with block scheduling, some of that time is recovered in the fewer times certain administrative procedures, such as taking attendance, must be done. Also, the longer contact per period that block scheduling provides allows entire lessons to be taught in one period instead of being stretched over two or three traditional periods. The more efficient use of class time certainly makes up a large portion of the lost minutes with the block scheduling format. The smaller class sizes that resulted from the use of block scheduling allowed for more individual attention, which also produced more efficient instruction.

Provisions were also made to help students adapt to the new scheduling procedure. All incoming freshmen are now required to take a study skills course. This class is designed to help the student adjust to high school, both socially and academically. In the early stages, this course functioned as a small study hall, with some instruction given to the students. It has now evolved into a separate department at North Charleston High School, with a diverse curriculum that addresses many needs of the students. Preparation for the state exit exams, monitoring of a student's progress in all classes, and career choice education now form part of the study skills class.

With the opportunity to take up to 32 Carnegie units of credit in 4 years of high school, many electives needed to be offered so that students could fill a schedule of eight class periods. North Charleston High School took time to develop many new electives and also expanded its college-level program. More than 10 new elective courses were developed, such as African American studies and multimedia technology, to meet the new course load demand. As the use of block scheduling progressed at North Charleston High School, some new electives were added and some were deleted. It was determined that varied and numerous electives had to be a part of the block scheduling program to avoid large study hall sections and large class sizes. Advanced Placement (AP) courses and college credit courses are a large part of the elective program. The social studies department added three college credit programs that attract a large number of seniors, decreasing study hall loads and early dismissal numbers. Two AP courses, calculus and chemistry, are taught every day to meet the minimum number of instructional minutes required by the College Board. The students are given a better chance of success in these difficult courses by meeting every day.

Another successful program that has developed out of the use of block scheduling is the ability to teach a "block" of students, allowing teachers to collaborate and teach lessons across the curriculum. A typical block is a group of 25 students that all follow the same exact schedule throughout a day. This allows up to four teachers to teach the same block of students. This concept has been successful in the gifted and talented program as well as "blocking" all at-risk students. To facilitate this program, the faculty is investigating the idea of a common planning period on one of the alternating days. It is hoped that this would allow a significant increase in teachers' ability to plan across the curriculum and team teach. An added benefit to common planning would be the reduction in study hall enrollment as students would be able to schedule seven classes instead of eight. Several obstacles exist to this common planning idea and it does not appear feasible for the near future.

North Charleston High School has been on the A/B block schedule for 4 years. The school has enjoyed many successes because of block scheduling. The flexibility that block scheduling provides has allowed many innovative ideas to evolve, and the students of North Charleston High School have certainly benefited.

⊞ 7 ⊞

Teaching in the Extended Period

When administrators conduct surveys to measure attitudes and actual changes in teacher behavior, the responses are remarkably consistent. The vast majority of teachers, usually in the 85% to 90% range, claim they like the change to block scheduling, and student surveys provide similar results. Both students and teachers also report that in most classes the teaching methods do substantially change to coincide with the demands of the extended class periods. If, then, we can assume that most teachers are ready and willing to make block scheduling a success in their school, the principal's responsibility to encourage these efforts is significant.

The survey I conducted that was published in the *Texas Study of Secondary Education* asked principals to identify the most difficult obstacles they had encountered in successfully implementing block scheduling. The most frequent response was to site the difficulty that many teachers had in adapting to the 90-minute period and the related problem of inadequate training to support teachers in the transition to block scheduling. Although teacher adaptation was clearly the most challenging problem according to respondents, several also identified concerns about new teachers and less capable teachers.

It is fundamental that principals must consider the teacher training aspect of block scheduling to be as important as the actual decision to restructure the schedule. It will not be sufficient to have a presentation about changing teaching strategies and then hope that teachers will figure out how to effectively modify their planning and teaching styles. Thomas L. Shortt and Yvonne V. Thayer observed that "block scheduling requires teachers to think differently about teaching; they need educational experiences that support an understanding of the block as well as training in appropriate teaching practices" (Shortt & Thayer, 1997, p. 11). Principals and curriculum leaders must work collaboratively with teachers to establish a continuing program of staff development. Teachers, like students, will have individualized needs based on their experiences, skills, and willingness to change. An effective staff development plan will take these factors into account and will promote growth that will extend and challenge the teacher's abilities. There are many practical ideas available to assist teachers in being more effective in a block schedule.

Segmenting Daily Lessons

One of the best methods of revising a teacher's approach to lesson planning is to promote segmenting the 90-minute class period into three to five separate units. Each segment should be approximately 25 minutes in length, and an effort should be made to utilize all available instructional time. A good step that principals can take to assist teachers in this change would be to provide a redesigned lesson plan book that clearly divides the class time into identifiable units.

Gig Harbor High School in Gig Harbor, Washington, is a school of about 1,400 students that implemented block scheduling several years ago. A team drawn from the professional staff consisting of Ken Brown, Daniel Dizon, Sherri Patterson, and Derek Sheffield surveyed teachers in an action research project to identify lesson formats used by teachers to engage students in their 100-minute class periods. The teacher survey data reported the following combinations as those most frequently used by the teachers.

- Warm up/opening activity
- Instruction/lecture
- Group or partner work
- Presentations

- Lecture/set up instructions
- Group work
- Reports/presentations
- Give/start homework assignment
- Lecture/instruction/guided practice
- Labs/activities with groups or partners
- Class discussion
- Handout/homework assignment (Marshak, 1997, p. 86)

Teachers should understand that these suggestions are not intended to be rigid rules that require each class every day to be equally divided into arbitrary instructional units. Such inflexibility would be contrary to the increased instructional freedom that the extended class periods offer both students and teachers. In some cases, a presentation such as a mock trial, or science labs, may require the entire 90 minutes for that one activity. Using the extended class to conduct play rehearsals, have practice debate rounds, and even short field trips will open up new and exciting uses of the school day.

Learning Strategies

There are numerous proven techniques and strategies that can be included in the daily lesson plan design. One of the most familiar is cooperative learning, and it provides teachers making the transition to block scheduling with a useful pedagogical tool. Cooperative learning activities ensure that the learning is student centered, rather than teacher centered, by having the students engage in projects and activities in groups or with partners. Even basic cooperative learning strategies may, however, be beyond the abilities of some teachers who have never used this technique. Moreover, some teachers may be reluctant to trade lecture time for group work. Some teachers who are resisting the transition to block scheduling may try to influence others, and negative attitudes can be destructive at a critical time of change. Principals can recount problems, often with more experienced teachers, with those who view cooperative learning as "cooperative cheating" or group "chat" time. Principals will need to provide adequate staff development opportunities and classroom materials and, in some cases, encourage teachers to observe other teachers and even attend workshops. Cooperative learning can be an exciting and dynamic activity for students when planned, organized, and implemented properly. Numerous books, articles, and other materials are readily available to help teachers who are willing to expand their professional repertoire.

Although there are many potential learning activities that work well in an extended class period, a few have proven themselves particularly productive. Even the use of videotapes can be transformed from trying to get the entire tape shown in a 45-minute class to an activity in which there is time to explain the context of the videotape prior to viewing and have a discussion after viewing. Student projects can take on an entirely new dimension as class time is available to work with students individually and in groups. One such project that teachers are finding interesting is the development of student portfolios, especially in English and study skills classes. Students are assisted in preparing a portfolio that represents their best work as well as learning how to present the material to create a positive impression. Teachers may also work with the students in producing introductory letters and résumés as a part of the portfolio project. This work can be displayed at open house or on other occasions that bring parents to the school.

Teachers will find the extended period is well suited to class presentations, debates, and simulation activities. Both individual and group presentations allow students to lead the learning exercise while also developing communication skills. The use of group debates can be very educational, and they do not need to follow interscholastic competitive debating formats; instead, they can be organized around a simple clash of opinion. These activities will be very compatible with the learning objectives in most social studies classes, and topics may be either historical or contemporary. The extended period will enhance simulation games and activities and, as block scheduling becomes the predominant school scheduling mode, the availability of materials can be expected to increase.

The extended periods will also give teachers an opportunity to promote other higher learning skills by allowing more time for application strategies. The possibility of projects and assignments that may involve the student in applying principles to authentic learning environments will be expanded. Teachers in block scheduling schools have demonstrated a greater interest in using support facilities, such as the library and computer labs. Science teachers have been among the most supportive of block scheduling as 90-minute periods allow more comprehensive lab experiments and demonstrations.

Many administrators have reported that with the implementation of block scheduling has come a heightened interest in interdisciplinary studies and team teaching. Although nothing in the traditional schedule would preclude these activities, the extended class period and the prevailing sense of reform create an atmosphere in which principals can expect to find teachers wanting to try new ideas. This rekindled interest can energize the teachers and may be one of the most exciting school improvement outcomes of the block scheduling process.

Help for Teachers

Regardless of the intervention strategies used by the principal, some teachers will have difficulty in changing their basic approach to teaching either because of attitudes or ineffectiveness. Assuming most of the teachers are making progress, principals may want to focus on those teachers who seem to need additional assistance. Experienced principals are already familiar with a wide range of methods to help teachers, such as evaluations and teacher mentors. Three more ways of helping struggling teachers might also prove valuable to principals. First, it can be very productive to have teachers observe other teachers in their field in schools that have been on extended class periods for several years. Principals are usually very receptive to having others visit their school, and they can arrange for your teacher to observe one or more of their best teachers. Second, continue to provide all teachers with new articles on block scheduling in general, as well as materials on teaching strategies in the block. With the growing interest and acceptance of block scheduling, we can reasonably anticipate that new books, articles, and classroom materials will be forthcoming on a monthly basis. Third, it may be necessary to send some teachers to workshops specializing in improving teaching skills in a block schedule. Although workshops can be somewhat expensive, the return on investment for students will make it worthwhile. Among the several workshops that I have attended, the workshop conducted by the Institute for Educational Development (800-260-8180) was one of the most valuable. Seminars by Robert L. Canady are also excellent, although the focus is more on understanding block scheduling; they might be more appropriate for administrators and teams investigating block scheduling for their schools.

Evaluating Block Scheduling

To some extent it is difficult for those who implement a change to maintain objectivity in evaluating the success of that change. Yet a block scheduling reform should be evaluated at various stages of the program. In anticipation of evaluation, it is suggested that the team leading the block scheduling initiative develop an evaluation instrument reflecting the goals that the team hoped would be attained. This method will deter the late development of an instrument designed to reflect any change as the intended change. Although some efforts at analyzing the results of block scheduling will be continuous, a comprehensive evaluation involving gathering empirical data and conducting surveys should probably be withheld until the third year of implementation is nearly completed.

Objective data should be the first measure of program success. Even if a particular indicator cannot be specifically linked to the longer class periods, an evaluation of a number of predetermined indicators should reveal if the school has been meeting its goals. Academic indicators should include both standardized test results, such as the SAT/ACT and state exit exams scores, as well as honor roll statistics and failure rates. Other objective measures might include the number of school disciplinary referrals, suspensions and expulsions, attendance rates, dropout rates, and average class size. In addition to these measures, principals should try to assess school climate issues. In doing so, it will be particularly useful if data are available from the school prior to the transition to block scheduling. A series of questions can be developed and responses can be plotted on a Likert scale, allowing respondents to select answers (usually on a scale of one to five) that reflect their attitudes concerning school climate issues. Some sample questions that might be included are as follows.

For students:

- Do you feel this school provides opportunities for a quality education?
- Do you have adequate time to complete homework?
- Do you have adequate time to study for tests?
- Do your teachers give you individualized assistance in class?
- Do you feel the school is committed to meeting your educational needs?
- Does the school offer a good selection of core academics and electives?
- Do you like the longer class periods with block scheduling?
- Would you prefer to return to traditional 50-minute classes?
- Do you think teachers have changed their teaching styles?
- Do you think the change to block scheduling has improved our school?

For teachers:

- Do you feel the school provides a program of quality education?
- Has block scheduling contributed to reduced discipline problems in the class?
- Has block scheduling improved the learning climate at our school?
- Are you able to provide students with more individualized instruction?
- Have you had adequate support in the transition to extended class periods?
- Do you favor the change to block scheduling?
- Would you prefer a traditional schedule of 50-minute classes?
- Has block scheduling had a positive effect on students?
- Do you feel block scheduling has been a good change for our school?
- Have you changed your teaching methods in the extended classes?

These questions are only samples; administrators would refine the questions to address campus concerns. Some descriptive information would be needed to be able to disaggregate data. Certainly, you would need to know if the student or teacher was new to the system or was a new teacher. Respondents could provide this information while still maintaining anonymity. By reviewing both objective and subjective data, administrators should be able to draw some conclusions about the success of block scheduling in their schools and consider what steps are needed to improve the process.

References

Marshak, D. (1997). *Action research on block scheduling.* Princeton, NJ: Eye On Education.

Shortt, T. L., & Thayer, Y. V. (1997, December). A vision for block scheduling: Where are we now? Where are we going? *NASSP Bulletin,* p. 11.

Suggested Reading

Barth, R. S. (1991, October). Restructuring schools: Some questions for teachers and principals. *Phi Delta Kappan,* pp. 123-128.

Hampton, D. (1997). *Strengthening your block schedule program: Practical teaching strategies for extended class periods.* Medina, WA: Institute for Educational Development.

Rettig, M. D., & Canady, R. L. (1997, February). All around the block schedule. *The Education Digest,* p. 31.

Vawter, D. H. (1997, May). *Welcome to block scheduling.* (World Wide Web: http://curry.edschool.virginia.edu/dhv3v/block/BSintro.html)

▦ 8 ▦

Overcoming Barriers to Implementation and Ensuring Success

It is very important for administrators and leadership teams to be well informed about the criticisms of block scheduling. At any point in the difficult task of building a consensus for change, opponents to the change may try to derail the reform effort. This response may be motivated by any number of reasons, but a vocal minority focusing on the contentious issues related to block scheduling may be able to defeat the initiative. We have already considered several problems that can result from block scheduling and how these problems can be countered, usually through scheduling. Nevertheless, there are some concerns that tend to be the focal point of discussions and they must be carefully examined in the process of adopting block scheduling for your school.

Achievement Issue

Although increased academic progress in terms of grades has been demonstrated repeatedly at block-scheduled schools, the question of improved achievement as measured by standardized tests is a more challenging proposition. Critics are adamant that block scheduling is either detrimental to improved achievement or that it has no positive impact on achievement scores. Kathy Mell claims that "in addition to the case studies previously mentioned, two extensive scientific studies are available that compare academic performance on the block versus traditional scheduling. Contrary to proponent's rhetoric, David Bateson's study, which examined all British Columbia 10th-grade students, showed that full-year students outperformed semester students (quoted in Mell, 1996, p. 2). Other studies by Raphael, Wahlstrom, and McLean (1986), which were conducted in the 1980s in Canadian schools, also made similar claims. A more recent study by Wronkovich, Hess, and Robinson (1997) examined the relationship between achievement scores on the Ohio Early Math Placement Test (EMPT) among students at blocked schools as compared to students in traditionally scheduled schools in Ohio school districts. Although the authors did qualify their claims, they concluded that "there have not yet been sufficient controlled longitudinal studies to lead to enthusiastic support for block scheduling. There may be problems for students in digesting larger quantities of math over a short period of time and the intervening lapses without math instructions" (p. 40). Other critics have continued to place the burden of proof on those seeking to change from traditional schedules. Jeff Lindsay observed that "if the hard data show that block scheduling or whole language or new math hurt academic performance, we have no right adopting those programs just because they're popular" (Lindsay, 1997, p. 34).

The issue of academic achievement is a challenging one that may never be resolved to a degree of certainty that would satisfy everyone. However, other studies have indicated that there is a positive relationship between block scheduling and achievement scores. The North Carolina Department of Public Instruction (1995) compared test scores of students on the 1995 End-of-Course exams in blocked schools versus traditionally scheduled schools. North Carolina has been a leader in restructuring, and well over 30% of its high schools were using block scheduling in 1995. The study reported that "after adjusting for starting point, parental education level, and homework time, the 1995 EOC test scores of blocked school groups in all five (required) courses—English 1, Algebra 1, ELP, biology, and U.S. history—were significantly higher than nonblocked schools" (p. 4).

Another study was conducted by Gary Wrinkle at Friendswood High School when he compared matching groups of students from five nonblocked schools with Friendswood students. He found that "Friendswood High School students outperformed the 'same-status' students in the five comparable nonblock high schools in the 10th grade on reading, writing, and mathematics sections of the TAAS tests" (Wrinkle, 1997, p. 40). Other studies have found the impact of block scheduling on achievement tests to be negligible, or insignificant. Susan L. Lockwood conducted a study to identify the relationship between achievement in algebra and geometry and block scheduling. She found no significant differences in achievement when block scheduling students were compared to traditionally scheduled students. She concluded that "without a decline in student achievement in each course, and the increased opportunity for students to take additional academic and technical courses, the overall achievement of students should be significantly high upon graduation on the semesterized block schedule compared to the six-period schedule" (Lockwood, 1995, p. 103).

In addition to the studies that have been conducted, educators who have investigated block scheduling are generally supportive of the proposition that student achievement increases. Dianne Hampton stated clearly that "there is an overall improvement in grades and more students make the honor roll. There are also better scores on standardized tests and exams for advanced placement" (Hampton, 1997, p. 21). Furthermore, administrators frequently report achievement gains in their schools following a block scheduling initiative. My own experience may be useful in illustrating the point. When I assumed the principalship at Rio Vista High School, the school had already committed to implementing an alternating block schedule. I had experience as an administrator in implementing block scheduling at my previous school and was able to help facilitate the transition. On my arrival, I found that the school's scores on the 10th-grade state exit exams were below state averages and the school's Texas Education Agency rating was "acceptable." In the following 2 years, the scores in each of three areas tested—writing, reading, and mathematics—have risen significantly and are above state averages. Our school has earned a TEA rating of "recognized." Like many other principals, I feel block scheduling was a key component in the success we have experienced with our students.

The clash of studies will probably never prove convincing to those on opposite ends of this issue, and continued research is certainly warranted. Both sides vigorously attack the methodologies and credibility of any study cited by the other side while overlooking any deficiencies or stated limitations of their own sources. The Canadian studies have often been quoted as proving the case against improved achievement with block scheduling. But others have disputed the Canadian studies as having little relevance to the current restructuring movement. David S. Hottenstein argues that

> comparing Canada's governmental education system to ours is a desperate apples-to-oranges contrast. Furthermore, Canada's block scheduling initiative 20 years ago was a top-down decision in the midst of teacher cuts and money problems and involved little or no training for teachers. At best, it is a convenient but unfair comparison. All of the so-called "Canadian studies" do not relate or align with the latest wave of block scheduling in the states. (Hottenstein, 1997, p. 2)

Other proponents of block scheduling have questioned the methodology of the Canadian studies and disputed the meaning of the data. In some cases, the claims made by those conducting the research are more restrained than the claims made by those who use the studies to support their viewpoint. For example, the authors of the Ohio math achievement study offered that "the team must caution the reader, however, not to make broad-based assumptions from this limited study. Some students may profit from intensified study; this impression came through in the qualitative research" (Wronkovich et al., 1997, p. 35).

It is a very difficult problem to attempt to establish cause and effect relationships between block scheduling and achievement scores on objective exams. Limiting the claims on both sides is the fact that there are so many variables operating that can distort the results of even the best tests. First, the very circumstance of a school being involved in restructuring efforts implies that there is a heightened interest in making changes to improve the school learning climate. While implementing block scheduling, principals and leadership teams may be incorporating numerous other strategies to promote student success. Teachers may be increasing efforts to fulfill newly clarified goals and missions while also working in team teaching situations or other innovative approaches to teaching and learning. How much of a school's improvement can be attributed to any one change? A second factor that will always be important is how well the block scheduling plan is implemented, not all administrators and teachers bring the same skills to the effort. Limited financial resources may seriously affect needed training for teachers and the ability to purchase other support materials.

In summary, the question of how much effect block scheduling actually has on student achievement is unclear. It would seem that there are some advantages that have been reported in many schools, and most students should benefit academically from extended class periods. However, critics should remember that the desirability of block scheduling is not dependent on any one factor and those schools that have made the transition continue to report a wide range of positive benefits for both students and staff.

Transfers

We have already considered the problem of transfer students to some extent, but the continuing fragmentation of scheduling models in schools guarantees that this will remain a very challenging problem for principals. Although the alternating block schedule and the traditional schedule are similar in pacing, neither of these two plans is aligned with the accelerated block or the trimester plan. Moreover, the accelerated block and the trimester are not aligned with each other, and even similar models may differ substantially from modified plans. The student who transfers very likely will be faced with entering a class at a different point in the curriculum and may also be scheduled into more, or fewer, classes than they had in their previous school. Although transfer students have always represented a problem in matching class schedules, the situation is getting worse for students who must transfer during the school year.

Most schools deal with transfers by trying to accommodate the student with the best schedule of classes possible even though the student may lose some time invested in coursework or may struggle to catch up in other classes. One idea that some schools have used is a transition class, often staffed by teachers volunteering some portion of their planning time to assist the new students. The Mississippi Department of Education (1996) evaluated block scheduling in that state, and one of the recommendations it reported was to "require students transferring into a 4 × 4 schedule from a traditional schedule to attend after-school or night sessions to catch up in key academic subject areas" (p. 3). These solutions could help administrators reduce the effects of transferring, but the problem will remain and there is no real method to eliminate it as long as school schedules lack uniformity.

Attendance

Schools with block scheduling usually report improved attendance as one of the benefits of the change. Even if overall attendance rates do improve or remain the same, a block schedule can seriously affect individual students who have too many absences. Because the 90-minute period is comparable to two class periods in a traditional schedule, each absence becomes more pronounced in terms of lost instructional time. In the case of a 4 × 4 block, a student who misses several days because of illness risks falling behind his or her peers, and some schools that have implemented the plan have reported increased failures the first year. In A/B block schedules, students who are chronically absent may establish a pattern of missing more days on the "A" or "B" day that has more difficult classes.

Several intervention strategies may help reduce this problem. First, clearly communicate to parents at orientations and with newsletters the seriousness of the attendance situation and then address students directly in groups or individually about the necessity of being in attendance as much as possible. As discussed earlier, explain to parents the importance of spreading regular doctor and dental appointments over the entire schedule. Principals will need to be sensitive to scheduling assemblies and athletic events during the same periods. The A/B block allows greater flexibility because the class periods are spread over 2 days. It will be critical for principals to closely monitor the attendance of individual students and to follow up with the full range of school responses.

Block scheduling should not be viewed as a panacea for all the challenges confronting our schools. It is clear that the important benefits far outweigh the problems, most of which are not entirely unique to block scheduling anyway. When administrators, teachers, and students agree that the change is a good one for their own school, it should be considered a persuasive testimony in support of block scheduling. J. Casey Hurley conducted a study to analyze teacher attitudes toward block scheduling in western North Carolina. The study reported that "the overall data, however, clearly support the conclusion that teachers see advantages that outweigh disadvantages." The study also noted that "teachers are aware of the time lost in class, but they are still overwhelmingly in favor of the block schedule" (Hurley, 1997, pp. 61-62). Teachers are the very core of our educational system. When these dedicated professionals offer their assessment of block scheduling, it should be respected and highly valued.

References

Hampton, D. (1997). *Strengthening your block schedule program: Practical teaching strategies for extended class periods.* Medina, WA: Institute for Educational Development.

Hottenstein, D. (1997). *Rebuttal of extreme negative views on block scheduling including the Canadian studies.* (World Wide Web: http://mciunix.mciu.k12.pa.us/hhhpag/block.html)

Hurley, J. C. (1997, December). The 4 × 4 block scheduling model: What do teachers have to say about it? *NASSP Bulletin,* pp. 61-62.

Lindsay, J. (1997, July 19). *The case against block scheduling.* (World Wide Web: http://www.athenet.net/jlindsay/Block.html)

Lockwood, S. L. (1995, December). Semesterizing the high school schedule: The impact on student achievement in algebra and geometry. *NASSP Bulletin,,* p. 103.

Mell, K. (1996). *Caution advised on block scheduling.* (World Wide Web: http://www.execpc.com/presswis/block.html)

Mississippi Department of Education. (1996). *Final report on modular/block scheduling presented to the Mississippi Board of Education.* Jackson, MS: Author.

North Carolina Department of Public Instruction. (1995). *Blocked scheduled high school achievement: Comparison of 1995 end-of-course test scores for blocked and non-blocked high schools.* (World Wide Web: http://www.dpi.state.nc.us/block_scheduling_report.html)

Raphael, D., Wahlstrom, M., & McLean, L. D. (1986). Debunking the semesterizing myth. *Canadian Journal of Education.*

Wrinkle, G. (1997, Summer). The ups and downs of accelerated block scheduling at Friendswood High School. *TASSP Summer Conference Materials,* p. 40.

Wronkovich, M., Hess, C. A., & Robinson, J. E. (1997, December). An objective look at math outcomes based on new research into block scheduling. *NASSP Bulletin*, p. 40.

⊞ 9 ⊞

Rescheduling Time
for More Effective Schools

Both teachers and administrators have become somewhat cynical about educational reform; each year seems to bring the latest in a series of answers to America's school problems. Many educators now assume a "wait and see" attitude about proposed changes. In some cases, the reform efforts have been abandoned because they have proven ineffective, unpopular, or have become attached to a broader political or social issue. Block scheduling, however, has repeatedly proven itself to be a desirable change for schools, a reform that results in numerous benefits for both students and teachers. Indeed, most of the many benefits that administrators and others attribute to block scheduling are unchallenged. Even the results of objective achievement measures would seem to slightly favor students on block schedules, but even if achievement gains cannot be conclusively proven, it is clear that students learn as much, even though there is less total instructional time available. Therefore, we must conclude that block scheduling is a more efficient delivery system for learning. Steve Kramer made the point by observing that students in the North Carolina study had less instructional time each semester "yet performed as well as they had before. In addition, under the block schedule, the students were able to enroll in additional classes, and teachers' planning time nearly doubled, from one roughly 50-minute period a day to one 90-minute period a day" (quoted in Summerfield, 1996, p. 2). The case for block scheduling is a strong one and although administrators should be prepared to be questioned about the change, the answers to the questions should prove satisfactory to most concerned stakeholders.

To some extent, block scheduling is an outgrowth of the greater demands made on both high schools and middle schools. When the curriculum was more limited and schools focused on a few core classes, the six-period traditional schedule could adequately address student needs. In recent years, states have significantly increased the academic requirements needed for students to fulfill graduation plans and for schools to maintain accreditation. Today's students must complete computer courses in order to be functional in technologies that barely existed when their parents were in high school. School districts often add courses designed to assist students in reaching local goals, such as study skills, extended mathematics classes, or additional credit requirements in some curricular areas. Moreover, everyone who has an interest in students from the local districts to the federal government wants a "world class educational system." The traditional schedule simply cannot provide the opportunities that students need to be successful in the 21st century.

As principals and leadership teams consider different schedules, it would be constructive to remember that the decision to adopt a block schedule should reflect a long-term commitment. It may be best to begin with a relatively simple block plan and then modify it according to demonstrated needs. There is no reason to assume that the block schedule plan you adopt for implementation is the one your school will be on in 5 or 10 years. Indeed, some schools may want to adopt an A/B block schedule because of its essential similarity to a traditional schedule but view it as a transitional step to a 4 × 4 block schedule plan. When they are modifying the block, just as when they initially adopted it, administrators must have a consensus from the faculty or the prospects for success are diminished.

One of the most rewarding outcomes of the block scheduling movement has been to observe the extent to which other educators have enthusiastically shared their time and information with other schools. Many schools have prepared handbooks about their experiences and results with block scheduling and have made those materials readily available to other educators. Campus leaders have shown a real willingness to share their successes with others in order to benefit the students of other districts. Having been involved in implementing block scheduling in two schools and having researched the subject extensively, I am sometimes asked, "What is the best possible schedule?" The answer is, of course, the one that best serves your students in attaining the goal of giving each child a quality educational opportunity. Nevertheless, the schedule below represents one that should be both very effective and expansive enough to allow for student needs.

4 × 4 Accelerated Block Schedule With One Daily Period for Athletics/Activities

Period 1—8:00-9:25 85 minutes

Period 2—9:30-11:00 90 minutes (5 extra minutes for announcements)

Period 3—11:05-1:15 130 minutes (includes two lunch shifts)
   1st lunch—11:05-11:50 45 minutes (includes time for two passing periods)
   1st lunch class time—11:50-1:15 85 minutes
   2nd lunch class time—11:05-11:50 45 minutes
   2nd lunch—11:50-12:35 45 minutes (includes time for two passing periods)
   2nd lunch class time—12:35-1:15 40 minutes

Period 4—1:20-2:45 85 minutes

Period 5—2:50-3:30 40 minutes (athletics/activities)

Such a schedule marginally reduces instructional time from 90 to 85 minutes. It also adds a daily period that should be used exclusively for athletics, study halls, and other activities that will not create an additional class preparation for teachers. Some, perhaps most, students could be dismissed at 2:45 if they were not involved in any activity at the period five daily time slot. But again, the best schedule is the one most suited to the needs of your students and the goals of your district.

The block scheduling process should be a positive one for almost everyone involved. Although it is essential that teachers change their teaching strategies, reports from schools—and research—indicate that the vast majority of teachers will prove to be very adaptable and do an excellent job in the classroom. Jim Staunton and Teresa Adams studied teacher attitudes concerning block scheduling and reported the comments of an English teacher with more than 20 years of experience. The teacher observed that

> block scheduling has given me the freedom to diversify my methods of instruction and improve the quality of my interaction with students. I have incorporated more performance-based, student-engaged projects into my assessment, which requires more student-teacher cooperation and exchange. Longer class periods provide the time needed for more meaningful discussions on our literature [and the time to] check for individual understanding, correct and return quizzes, and provide time for dramatization or active learning strategies. (quoted in Staunton & Adams, 1997, p. 82)

This teacher spoke for many teachers, as well as students, who have found block scheduling to be an educational reform that has significantly improved the learning dynamics in high schools and middle schools.

References

Staunton, J., & Adams, T. (1997, December). What do teachers in California have to say about block scheduling? *NASSP Bulletin*, p. 82.
Summerfield, M. (1966, May 22). Research spans the spectrum on block scheduling. *Education Week on the Web*, p. 2.

Suggested Reading

Staunton, J. (1997, December). A study of teacher beliefs on the efficacy of block scheduling. *NASSP Bulletin*, pp. 73-80.

Resource A

Sample Schedules

One of the most valuable resources available to administrators and leadership teams is sample block schedules. These schedules are most useful because they reflect the product of the decision-making process in other schools, and in some cases they have been revised in order to solve some problem that existed in the initial schedule. Planners can study these schedules and determine whether or not they would be appropriate for use in their schools.

Some schedules reflect compromises that may be unique to a particular school or state. The number of lunch shifts will vary among schools and, with a few adjustments, an attractive schedule can be adapted to provide for more shifts. (Surprisingly, many large schools have only one lunch shift.) Other adjustments in starting or ending times may be needed because of bus route times. Many of the schools had assembly schedules in their packets; however, those are not included in this information. Modifying the regular schedule for assemblies will not be difficult.

No attempt has been made to put the schedules into a common format. The schedules are as the schools sent them, and each appears understandable even though some aspects of the schedules are illustrated differently. A few of the schedules were not provided by schools and are composites of several ideas. Some brief comments are provided, although most are self-explanatory.

4 × 4 Block Schedule

Period	Time	Minutes
1	7:30-8:55	85
Pass	8:55-9:05	10
2	9:05-10:30	85
Pass	10:30-10:40	10
3 Lunch	10:40-12:35	115
Pass	12:35-12:45	10
4	12:45-2:10	85

Comments: This schedule would be well suited to a large school requiring long passing periods and multiple lunch shifts. The early release time would also allow for the development of enrichment classes or athletics. In this schedule, a decision has been made to trade some instructional time for longer passing periods and an early release time—a loss of 5 minutes per class period.

SOURCE: University of Minnesota, Center for Applied Research and Educational Improvement.

Mansfield High School: 4 × 4 Block Schedule

Period 1	7:25-8:55	(90 Minutes)
Period 2	9:10-10:40	(90 Minutes)
Period 3	10:50-12:20	(90 Minutes)
Lunch	12:20-1:00	(40 Minutes)
Period 4	1:10-2:45	(95 Minutes)

Comments: Very much a good basic 4 × 4 block schedule. The start time is very early and the entire schedule could easily be moved back to a later start, or an additional daily period could be added after 2:45. This school was an early leader in implementing the accelerated block and has provided information and workshops for other schools.

SOURCE: Mansfield High School, Mansfield, Texas.

Asheboro High School: 4 × 4 Block Schedule

Period 1	8:00-9:30
Period 2	9:40-11:10
Period 3	11:20-12:50
Lunch	12:50-1:25
Period 4	1:30-3:00

Comments: A good basic schedule that reflects standard starting times. Schedules such as these are often good models to begin with as they are relatively simple to administer. There is also ample time available to increase the number of lunch shifts as needed.

SOURCE: Asheboro High School, Asheboro, North Carolina.

Jefferson Davis High School: 4 × 4 Block Schedule

Period 1	8:00-9:30	90 minutes
Period 2	9:45-11:15	90 minutes
Lunch	11:15-12:15	60 minutes
Period 3	12:15-1:45	90 minutes
Period 4	2:00-3:30	90 minutes

Comments: An interesting schedule that reflects concerns for students being in longer classes. Ample time is given between classes to get ready for the next class. This schedule is very simple and looks easy to implement, but 15-minute passing periods are probably too long. The school handbook indicates that the hour-long lunch period provided to students is also used for tutorials and club meetings.

SOURCE: Jefferson Davis High School (no location indicated in materials).

Joshua High School: A/B Block

Period 1/5	8:00-9:30	90 minutes
Period 2/6	9:35-11:15	100 minutes (to allow for announcements)
Period 3/7	11:20-1:30	130 minutes (to accommodate two lunch shifts)
1st Lunch	11:20-11:50	30 minutes
2nd Lunch	12:50-1:30	40 minutes
Period 4/8	1:35-3:05	90 minutes
Tutorial/ activities	3:05-3:30	25 minutes

Comments: This is a good A/B schedule; it should work well in most schools. The time allocated at the end of the day (3:05) can provide many opportunities for meeting the needs of students.

SOURCE: Joshua High School, Joshua, Texas.

McNeil High School: A/B Block

Period 1/5	9:05-10:35	90 minutes
Period 2/6	10:40-12:15	95 minutes (5 extra minutes for announcements)
Period 3/7	12:20-2:30	130 minutes (to accommodate four lunch shifts)
A.	Lunch	12:15-12:55
	Class	1:00-2:30
B.	Class	12:20-12:50
	Lunch	12:50-1:25
	Class	1:30-2:30
C.	Class	12:20-1:20
	Lunch	1:20-1:55
	Class	2:00-2:30
D.	Class	12:20-1:50
	Lunch	1:50-2:30
Period 4/8	2:35-4:05	90 minutes

Comments: McNeil High has been a leader in Texas, and has conducted workshops to help other schools construct block scheduling programs. McNeil is a large school, and the number of lunch shifts demonstrates use of the schedule to solve a crowded lunch situation. The schedule itself is a good basic plan, and the start time could easily be moved back to meet the needs of other schools.

SOURCE: McNeil High School, Round Rock, Texas.

Greenfield-Central High School: A/B Block Schedule

Time	Monday	Tuesday	Wednesday	Thursday	Friday
7:45-9:25 *100 minutes*	Blue 1	Gold 1	Blue 1	Gold 1	Blue 1
9:32-11:07 *95 minutes*	Blue 2	Gold 2	Blue 2	Gold 2	Blue 2
11:13-1:18 *95 + 30 minutes*	Blue 3	Gold 3	Blue 3 (includes lunch)	Gold 3	Blue 3
1:25-3:00 *95 minutes*	Blue 4	Gold 4	Blue 4	Gold 4	Blue 4

Comments: A good schedule that allows for longer periods than the usual 90 minutes in blocks. This school has allowed for 6-minute passing periods, and many principals would agree that the standard 5-minute period is too short. The lunch time allowed seems short, but if we assume that the ending time could be moved all the way to 3:30, this could be easily modified.

SOURCE: Greenfield-Central High School, Greenfield, Indiana.

Alternating Block Schedule: Composite for Large Schools

8:00-9:30	Period 1A/5B
9:36-11:00	Period 2A/6B
Period 3A/7B Lunch	
11:11-11:48	1st lunch shift
12:05-12:39	2nd lunch shift
12:47-1:24	3rd lunch shift
Period 3A/7B Class periods	
11:54-1:24	Class period for students with 1st lunch
11:17-12:05	Split class for students with 2nd lunch
11:17-12:47	Class time for students with 3rd lunch
1:30-3:00	Period 4A/8B

Comments: This schedule would reflect the needs of a large school that needed longer passing periods and multiple lunch shifts to accommodate students. Otherwise, it is a good workable A/B block. It also has an earlier enough ending time to allow for other possibilities, such as an activity period or tutoring.

SOURCE: Blair Lybbert in *Texas Study of Secondary Education.*

J. L. Mann High School: A/B Block—Activity Schedule

Period 1	8:30-9:55	85 minutes (allow extra 5 min. for announcements)	
Activity period	10:00-10:40	40 minutes	
Period 2	10:45-12:05	80 minutes	
Period 3	12:05-12:40	1st lunch shift	35 minutes
	12:45-2:05	1st lunch class	35 minutes
	12:45-1:20	2nd lunch shift	35 minutes
	1:20-2:05	2nd lunch class	45 minutes
Period 4	2:10-3:30	80 minutes	

Comments: This was the alternate/activity schedule sent by this school. On examination, however, it could provide an interesting schedule for a school willing to cut back the instructional time and provide a daily activity or homeroom period.
SOURCE: J. L. Mann High School, Greenville, North Carolina.

Abell Junior High School: Modified A/B Block

Period 1/2	8:40-10:25	105 minutes
Period 3/4	10:30-12:15	105 minutes
Lunch	12:20-12:45	25 minutes
Period 5	12:50-1:45	55 minutes (meets every day)
Period 6/7	1:50-3:40	110 minutes

Comments: This block provides for a seven-period day rather than eight periods. The start time is late enough that a "zero" period could also be added, restricted to certain electives, perhaps band. Materials from this school indicate that the 55-minute daily period is used for electives, PE, study skills, and computer literacy classes.
SOURCE: Abell Junior High School, Midland, Texas.

Olney High School: Modified A/B Block Schedule

Period 1/5	8:05-9:35	90 minutes
Period 2/6	9:40-11:10	90 minutes
Period 3/7	11:15-12:45	90 minutes
Lunch	12:45-1:25	40 minutes
Period 4/8	1:30-3:00	90 minutes
Period 9	3:05-4:00	55 minutes (meets every day)

Comments: A well-structured schedule that allows for the full 90-minute classes while still providing a daily period to meet other needs. It is, however, a long school day, and a schedule like this should probably allow for early release and late arrivals to school. A cautionary note on this schedule: It would be tempting to fill the ninth period with regular a academic class, especially as it is 55 minutes long. To use the period in this manner would create additional teacher preparations, and it would be contrary to the principles supporting extended periods.
SOURCE: Olney High School, Olney, Texas.

Rio Vista High School: Modified A/B Block Schedule

8:00-9:20	Period 1A/5B
9:25-10:45	Period 2A/6B
10:50-12:10	Period 3A/7B
Period 4A/8B Lunch	
12:10-12:45	1st lunch shift
12:50-1:20	2nd lunch shift
Period 4A/8B Class time	
12:50-2:10	Class time for 1st lunch students
12:15-12:50/1:25-2:10	Split class for 2nd lunch students
2:15-2:30	Activity period/homeroom
2:40-3:30	Period 9 (athletics/special classes)

Comments: This schedule works well but has a lot of class periods over 2 days. The nine periods have resulted in few class conflicts and a wide range of electives available to students. Again, as with other schedules, planners should avoid the temptation to use the daily period as a regular academic time slot.

SOURCE: Rio Vista High School, Rio Vista, Texas.

L. D. Bell High School: Trimester Schedule

7:45 a.m.	Teachers arrive for tutorial in their rooms		
8:15-9:29	Period 1	A lunch	10:55-11:34
9:35-10:49	Period 2	A class	11:40-12:54
10:55-12:54	Period 3/lunch		
1:00-2:14	Period 4	B lunch	12:15-12:54
2:20-3:34	Period 5	B class	10:55-12:09

Comments: This trimester reflects the shorter than 90-minute period classes needed in the trimester plan. This school has been a leader in trimester scheduling.

SOURCE: L. D. Bell High School, Hurst, Texas.

Cleburne High School: Trimester Schedule

REGULAR BELL SCHEDULE		
Pass	8:04-8:10	
Period 1	8:10-9:25	75 minutes
Pass	9:25-9:31	

Announcements	9:31-9:36	
Period 2	9:36-10:51	75 minutes
Pass	10:51-10:57	
Period 3/lunch	10:57-12:48	111 minutes
Pass	12:48-12:54	
Period 4	12:54-2:09	75 minutes
Pass	2:09-2:15	
Period 5	2:15-3:30	75 minutes

LUNCH SCHEDULE

A lunch	10:57-11:34	37 minutes (return bell at 11:28)
Class	11:34-12:48	74 minutes
B class	10:57-11:34	37 minutes
Lunch	11:34-12:11	37 minutes (return bell at 12:05)
B class	12:11-12:48	37 minutes
C class	10:57-12:11	74 minutes
Lunch	12:11-12:48	37 minutes

Comments: A well-designed basic trimester that accommodates multiple lunch shifts.

SOURCE: Cleburne High School, Cleburne, Texas.

Southwestern High School:
4 × 4 Block Schedule With Flex Period

	Monday, Wednesday, Friday	
1st	8:30-10:00	90 minutes
2nd	10:05-11:35	90 minutes
3rd	11:40-1:30	90 minutes (plus 20-minute lunch)
	10-minute break	
4th	1:40-3:10	90 minutes
	Tuesday	
1st	8:30-9:45	75 minutes
Flex	9:50-10:20	30 minutes
2nd	10:25-11:35	70 minutes
3rd	11:40-1:30	90 minutes (plus 20-minute lunch)
	10-minute break	
4th	1:40-3:10	90 minutes
	Thursday	
1st	8:30-10:00	90 minutes
2nd	10:05-11:35	90 minutes
3rd	11:40-1:20	80 minutes (plus 20-minute lunch)

Flex	1:25-1:55	30 minutes
4th	2:00-3:10	70 minutes

Comments: This schedule provides a typical M-W-F and a different schedule for T-T in order to allow teachers to address specific concerns. The "flex" time could be used for tutorials or activities needed to meet campus objectives.

SOURCE: Southwestern High School, Somerset, Kentucky.

Hico Secondary School: Traditional Schedule on Monday to Wednesday Followed by A/B on Thursday and Friday

Monday Tuesday Wednesday		Thursday Friday	
Breakfast	7:30-7:55	Breakfast	7:30-7:55
1	8:00-8:50	1/2	8:00-9:20
2	8:55-9:45	3/4	9:25-10:45
Tutorial	9:50-10:20	5/6	10:50-12:10
3	10:25-11:15	Lunch	12:10-12:45
4	11:20-12:10	7 (Thursday)	12:50-2:15
Lunch	12:10-12:45	8 (Friday)	12:50-2:15
5	12:50-1:40		
6	1:45-2:35		
7	2:40-3:30		

**Thursday 2:15-4:00: Campus-level curriculum development and interdisciplinary planning
**Friday 2:15-4:00: Districtwide planning and staff development

Comments: An interesting schedule that allows for schoolwide early dismissal on Thursday and Friday. This school indicates that the early release time is used for campus- or district-level planning and curriculum design.

SOURCE: Hico High School, Hico, Texas.

A/B Block With Enrichment Period

	Monday	*Tuesday*	*Wednesday*	*Thursday*	*Friday*
7:35-9:00	1	2	1	2	1
9:09-10:34	3	Enrichment	3	Enrichment	3
10:43-12:38	5	4	5	4	5
12:45-2:10	7	6	7	6	7

(Week 2 is the opposite of Week 1)

Comments: This schedule is basically an eight-period block, except that the "enrichment" class is not a regular class. Information with the schedule indicates that it is used for such purposes as enrichment, activities, remediation, or assemblies. This schedule would seem to provide a good basic block with one period available to be used to pursue campus goals.

SOURCE: University of Minnesota, Center for Applied Research and Educational Improvement.

Modified Block Plan With 1 Day of Short Periods

MONDAY SCHEDULE
Period 1   7:40-8:25
Period 2   8:30-9:15
Period 3   9:20-10:05
Period 4   10:10-11:30
    1st lunch   10:05-10:40
    2nd lunch   10:55-11:30
Period 5   11:35-12:20
Period 6   12:25-1:10
Period 7   1:15-2:00
Period 8   2:05-2:50
    TUESDAY THROUGH FRIDAY (A/B ALTERNATING)
Period 1/5   7:40-9:10
Period 2/6   9:17-10:47
Period 3/7   10:54-1:04
    1st lunch   10:47-11:27
    2nd lunch   12:24-1:04
Period 4/8   1:11-2:40

Comments: This schedule reflects the concern that teachers have on A/B schedules of not having enough access to their students. This alternative is one that is commonly discussed but usually rejected because of a sense that the short periods will not be long enough to be used constructively. If the leadership team that implements a hybrid schedule can effectively plan for the 45-minute classes, the schedule might be able to provide solutions to problems unique to a given school.

SOURCE: Trimble Tech High School, Fort Worth, Texas.

Resource B

Selected Bibliography
on Block Schedules

Adams, D. C., & Salvaterra, M. E. (1997). *Block scheduling: Pathways to success.* Lancaster, PA: Technomic.

Alam, D., & Seick, R. E. (1994, May). A block schedule with a twist. *Phi Delta Kappan.*

Barth, R. S. (1991, October). Restructuring schools: Some questions for teachers and principals. *Phi Delta Kappan.*

Brett, M. (1996, September). Teaching block scheduled class periods. *The Education Digest,* p. 37.

Bruckner, M. (1997, December). Eavesdropping on change: Listening to teachers during the first year of an extended block schedule. *NASSP Bulletin,* pp. 42-52.

Canady, R. L. (1996). *Teaching in the block: Strategies for engaging learning.* Princeton, NJ: Eye on Education.

Canady, R. L., & Rettig, M. (1993, December). Unlocking the lockstep high school schedule. *Phi Delta Kappan.*

Canady, R. L., & Rettig, M. (1995). *Block scheduling: A catalyst for change in high schools.* Princeton, NJ: Eye on Education.

Carroll, J. M. (1990, January). The Copernican Plan: Restructuring the American high school. *Phi Delta Kappan.*

Carroll, J. M. (1994a). *The Copernican Plan evaluated: The evolution of a revolution.* Topsfield, MA: Copernican Associates.

Carroll, J. M. (1994b, March). Organizing time to support learning. *The School Administrator,* p. 27.

Cawelti, G. (1993, Summer). Restructuring large high schools to personalize learning for all. *ERS Spectrum*, pp. 20-21.

Cawelti, G. (1994). *High school restructuring: A national study.* Arlington, VA: Education Research Service.

Center for Applied Research and Educational Improvement. (1995a). *Block scheduling questions and answers.* Minneapolis: University of Minnesota.

Center for Applied Research and Educational Improvement. (1995b). *Introduction to block scheduling.* Minneapolis: University of Minnesota.

Center for Applied Research and Educational Improvement. (1995c). *Report study of the four-period schedule for Amoka-Hennepin District No. 11.* Minneapolis: University of Minnesota.

Dempsey, R. A., & Traverso, H. P. (1983). *Scheduling the secondary school.* Reston, VA: NASSP.

Edwards, C. M., Jr. (1993, May). Restructuring to improve student performance. *NASSP Bulletin,* p. 78.

Fogarty, R. J. (1995). *Think about . . . block scheduling.* Palatine, IL: Skylight Training and Publishing.

Gerkin, J. L. (1995, April). Building block schedules: A firsthand assessment of restructuring the school day. *The Science Teacher.*

Hackman, D. G. (1995, November). Ten guidelines for implementing block scheduling. *Educational Leadership,* pp. 24-27.

Hampton, D. (1997). *Strengthening your block schedule program: Practical teaching strategies for extended class periods.* Medina, WA: Institute for Educational Development.

Hinn, D. M. (1996, April 12). *VMEA block scheduling statement.* Blacksburg, VA: Virginia Music Education Association.

Hurley, J. C. (1997a, December). The 4 × 4 block scheduling model: What do students have to say about it? *NASSP Bulletin,* p. 65.

Hurley, J.C. (1997b, December). The 4 × 4 block scheduling model: What do teachers have to say about it? *NASSP Bulletin,* pp. 61-62.

Kruse, G., & Zulkoski, M. (1997, December). The Northwest experience: A lesser road traveled. *NASSP Bulletin,* pp. 16-22.

Lenz, B. (1997, November). Block scheduling and student activities. *Leadership,* pp. 27-28. (NASSP)

Lockwood, S. (1995, December). Semesterizing the high school schedule: The impact on achievement in algebra and geometry. *NASSP Bulletin,* p. 103.

Lybbert, B. (1996, Fall). Block scheduling: Considerations for adoption and implementation. *Texas Study of Secondary Education,* p. 20.

Marshak, D. (1997). *Action research on block scheduling*. Princeton, NJ: Eye on Education.

McClaran, N. (1994, April). Re-examining curriculum. *Texas Association for Curriculum and Development*, p. 1.

Miller, E. (1992, March-April). Breaking the tyranny of the schedule. *Harvard Education Newsletter*, p. 6.

Mississippi Department of Education. (1996, April). *Final report on modular/block scheduling presented to the Mississippi Board of Education*. Jackson, MS: Author.

Mistretta, G. M., & Polansky, H. B. (1997, December). Prisoners of time: Implementing a block schedule in the high school. *NASSP Bulletin*, p. 29.

National Education Commission on Time and Learning. (1994). *Prisoners of time: Report of the National Education Commission on Time and Learning*. Washington, DC: Government Printing Office.

Raphael, D., Wahlstrom, M., & McLean, L. D. (1986). Debunking the semesterizing myth. *Canadian Journal of Education*.

Rettig, M. D., & Canady, R. L. (1997, February). All around the block. *The School Administrator*, p. 31.

Schoenstein, R. (1994, February). Making block scheduling work. *Virginia Journal of Education*, pp. 16-19.

Shanahan, L. (1997, November). Survival of activities in a block scheduling format. *Leadership*, p. 28. (NASSP)

Shortt, T. L., & Thayer, Y. V. (1995). What can we expect to see in the next generation of block scheduling? *NASSP Bulletin*, p. 40.

Shortt, T. L., & Thayer, Y. V. (1997, December). A vision for block scheduling: Where are we now? Where are we going? *NASSP Bulletin*, p. 11.

Smith, R. (1996, July). Block that schedule. *The Executive Educator*, p. 40.

Staunton, J. (1997a, December). A study of teacher beliefs on the efficacy of block scheduling. *NASSP Bulletin*, pp. 73-80.

Staunton, J., & Adams, T. (1997b, December). What do teachers in California have to say about block scheduling? *NASSP Bulletin*, p. 82.

Summerfield, M. (1996, May 22). Research spans the spectrum on block scheduling. *Education Week on the Web*.

Traverso, H. P. (1991, October). Scheduling from micro to macro. *The Practitioner*, pp. 1-8. (NASSP)

Ubben, G. C., & Hughes, L. W. (1987). *The principal*. Boston: Allyn & Bacon.

Wronkovich, M., Hess, C. A., & Robinson, J. E. (1997, December). An objective look at math outcomes based on new research into block scheduling. *NASSP Bulletin*, p. 40.